ENGLISH FURNITURE
1550-1760

ENGLISH FURNITURE 1550-1760

GEOFFREY WILLS

DOUBLEDAY & COMPANY, INC.,
GARDEN CITY,
NEW YORK.

Other Books in this Series

ENGLISH AND IRISH GLASS (1968)
by Geoffrey Wills
SBN 85112 117 9

ENGLISH POTTERY AND PORCELAIN (1969)
by Geoffrey Wills
SBN 85112 145 4

ANTIQUE FIREARMS (1969)
by Frederick Wilkinson
SBN 85112 164 0

EDGED WEAPONS (1970)
by Frederick Wilkinson
SBN 85112 171 3

BATTLE DRESS (1970)
(A Gallery of Military Style and Ornament)
by Frederick Wilkinson
SBN 85112 172 1

BRITISH GALLANTRY AWARDS (1971)
by P. E. Abbott and J. M. A. Tamplin
SBN 85112 173 X

ENGLISH FURNITURE, 1760–1900 (1971)
by Geoffrey Wills
SBN 85112 175 6

Published in Great Britain by
GUINNESS SUPERLATIVES LTD.,
2 CECIL COURT, LONDON ROAD, ENFIELD, MIDDLESEX
Printed in 10pt. Century Series 227
by McCorquodale Printers Limited, London.
Monotone and 4-colour half-tone blocks by Gilchrist Bros. Ltd., Leeds.

CONTENTS

ADDENDA

page 168   John Hervey recorded the following payments in 1702:
        April 30. Paid Gumley for my bureau & some china ware   *£11 10 0*
        Dec. 16. Paid Peter Gumley for China & Japan ware   *£29 0 0*
        Heal suggested that Peter Gumley was perhaps the husband of Mrs. Elizabeth
        Gumley and father of John.

INTRODUCTION

THE large quantity of old English furniture surviving today is often a cause of comment, as it does not tally with all modern appraisals of the past. The picture painted by some sentimentalists and others is of a Ye Olde England in which most of the inhabitants dragged out a miserable gin-soaked existence in sparsely-furnished hovels, while in contrast a few rapacious landlords lived in splendour amid the finest productions of the underpaid craftsmen of the time. In fact, there were poor people and there were rich ones, but the majority lived probably somewhere in between these opposite poles, and confirmation of this surely lies in the vast remaining amounts of furniture from their homes. Also, judging by the impressively large quantity of high-quality specimens, there must have been a greater number of men of wealth and taste than is usually admitted.

It was these men who stimulated the introduction of fresh styles of design and construction by demanding greater visual and creature comforts. Their example inspired the average householder, whose requirements were tempered not only by personal variations of income and taste but by his immediate surroundings. With a more modest style of living, his standards were less exacting.

A book devoted to the subject of furniture, while it does not ignore the more ordinary productions must largely concentrate on the finest of each period. By this means, the reader is given yardsticks against which to judge other pieces.

Knowledge of the past can only be partial; with the passage of time it becomes progressively more difficult to learn of what occurred. Memory is capricious, and only a small percentage of daily happenings is ever committed to paper with accuracy. Regarding artifacts, the surroundings of our ancestors can, in the main, only be gauged by what has been preserved by sheer chance, and it may be suspected that such remains are not always fully representative specimens. Many of them are in museums and private collections on both sides of the Atlantic and are fully documented, but the list is always lengthening as unsuspected treasures come to light.

Interest in old furniture of all countries has greatly increased during the past few years and research into it has been immensely, some would say belatedly, stimulated. The Furniture History Society,[1] which was founded in 1964, has brought together many of those seeking more knowledge and its annual publication, *Furniture History*, is already an important forum for discussion of the furniture itself and its designers and makers.

Despite the fact that the publisher has generously allowed me two good-sized illustrated volumes, there have been difficult decisions to make as to what must be included or omitted. Within this understandable restriction I have endeavoured to embrace the widest possible field, and give the reader a maximum of information on a maximum of aspects of the subjects.

The importance of design cannot be overstated, but it stands or falls according to the skill of the craftsman. An appreciation of his standard of excellence is essential in forming a sound judgement, and it is hoped that the volumes will assist in its attainment.

G. W.

[1] *Details of membership are obtainable from: The Secretary, Furniture History Society, c/o Department of Furniture and Woodwork, Victoria and Albert Museum, London, S.W.7.*

BIBLIOGRAPHY

LIST OF BOOKS CITED

(Published in London unless otherwise stated)

W. Adam
The Gem of the Peak, 4th edition, 1845.

E. K. Chambers
The Elizabethan Stage, 4 vols., Oxford, 1923.

Anthony Coleridge
Chippendale Furniture, 1968.

H. M. Colvin
A Biographical Dictionary of English Architects, 1954.

Daniel Defoe
Tour Through Great Britain, 1727, re-published in 2 vols., 1927.

Averyl Edwards
Frederick Louis, Prince of Wales, 1947.

Ralph Edwards and Margaret Jourdain
Georgian Cabinet-Makers, 3rd edition, 1955.

John Evelyn
Sylva, or a Discourse of Forest Trees, 1664.
Diary and Correspondence, ed. H. B. Wheatley, 4 vols., 1906.

Celia Fiennes
Through England on a Side Saddle in the Time of William and Mary, 1888 (*The Journeys of Celia Fiennes*, ed. C. Morris, 1947).

John Gloag
A Short Dictionary of Furniture, revised ed., 1966.

Nicholas Goodison
English Barometers 1680–1860, 1969.

G. B. Harrison and P. A. Jones (trans.)
A Journal of All that was Accomplished by Monsieur de Maisse, Nonesuch Press, 1923.

William Harrison
Description of England, ed. L. Withington, N. D.

Ambrose Heal
London Furniture Makers, 1660–1840, 1953.

John Hervey, first Earl of Bristol
Diary, ed. S. H. A. H., Wells, 1894.

Randle Holme
Academy of Armory, Roxburghe Club, 1905.

Hugh Honour
Chinoiserie: A Vision of Cathay, 1961.

Margaret Jourdain
English Decoration and Furniture of the Early Renaissance, 1924.
The Works of William Kent, 1948.
Stuart Furniture at Knole, 1952.

Margaret Jourdain and R. Soame Jenyns
Chinese Export Art, 1950.

S. A. Khan
East India Trade in the Seventeenth Century, Oxford, 1923.

Francis Lenygon (pseud. Margaret Jourdain)
Furniture in England from 1660–1760, 1914.

Princess Marie Liechtenstein
Holland House, 2 vols., 1874.

Martin Lister
A Journey to Paris in the Year 1698, 1699.

J. C. Loudon
Encyclopaedia of Cottage, Farm and Villa Architecture and Furniture, 1829.

John Lowthorp
The Philosophical Transactions ... Abridg'd, 3 vols., 1705.

Percy Macquoid and Ralph Edwards
The Dictionary of English Furniture, 2nd, revised by Ralph Edwards, 3 vols., 1954.

Robert Manwaring
The Chair-Maker's Guide, 1765, reprinted 1937.

W. Matthews (ed.)
The Diary of Dudley Ryder, 1939.

Peter Osbeck
A Voyage to China and the East Indies, 2 vols., 1771.

Samuel Pepys
Diary, ed. Richard, Lord Braybrooke, 1854.

W. H. Quarrell and Margaret Mare (trans. and ed.)
London in 1710, from the Travels of Z. C. von Uffenbach, 1934.

William Salmon
Polygraphice, 8th edition, 1701

Henry Shaw
Specimens of Ancient Furniture, 1836.

John Stalker and George Parker
A Treatise of Japanning and Varnishing, 1688, reprinted 1960.

Margaret H. Swain
Historical Needlework, 1970.

R. W. Symonds
The Present State of Old English Furniture, 1921.
English Furniture from Charles II to George II, 1929.
Furniture-making in 17th and 18th Century England, 1955.

J. C. Timbs
Curiosities of London, 1868.

Horace Walpole
Anecdotes of Painting in England, ed. James Dallaway and R. N. Wornum, 3 vols., 1876.

P. Ward-Jackson
English Furniture Designs of the Eighteenth Century, 1958.

E. K. Waterhouse
Painting in Britain 1530–1790, 1953.

Geoffrey Wills
English Looking-Glasses, 1965.

PERIODICALS CITED

Apollo
The Burlington Magazine
The Connoisseur
Country Life

Furniture History
The Gentleman's Magazine
The London Magazine

1 : Elizabeth I

Tables, Chairs

THE forty-five years, 1558 to 1603, during which Queen Elizabeth I occupied the throne of England saw a substantial rise in the wealth and living-standards of the people. Her father, Henry VIII, had been a patron of the arts with a predilection for Italians, who came at his behest to provide him with the fashionable outward show of royalty. The model for such display was François I, King of France, who employed, among others, Benvenuto Cellini, and whose reign was notable in architecture for the building of Chambord, St. Germain and Fontainebleau.

The intervening reigns of Edward VI and Mary Tudor, totalling eleven years, saw little or no advance, but by the second half of Elizabeth's sovereignty one of her subjects was able to give a glowing account of daily life at the time. The man in question, William Harrison, penned his *Description of England* between 1577 and 1587, and it was incorporated in Ralph Holinshed's *Chronicles*, published in the latter year. Harrison wrote of the external appearance of many of the mansions, which contrasted with the ornamentation of their interiors, stating that

> ... many of our greatest houses have outwardly been very simple and plain to sight, which inwardly have been able to receive a duke with his whole train, and lodge them at their ease.

He noted that most of the buildings were constructed of timber, 'in framing whereof our carpenters have been and are worthily preferred before those of like science among all other nations'. Recently-built dwellings he added, were of 'brick and hard stone, or both, their rooms large and comely'.

Fig. 1: Elizabethan 'cup and cover' table-leg, the lower part carved with acanthus leaves, round the centre a band of bosses, and the top with scrolls and leaves on a punched ground. Above is an Ionic capital. (Buckland Abbey, Devon: City Museum and Art Gallery, Plymouth.)

It was a time of widespread building activity, and the great country mansions, 'the cloud capp'd towers, the gorgeous palaces' of Woollaton, Hardwick, Burghley and Longleat stand as evidence. They are reminders of the scale on which the noblemen lived and by which, so the envious remarked, they ostentatiously displayed their wealth. Less pretentious houses have also survived, but most of them have been so altered over the centuries that their original appearance can usually only be imagined.

Left, *Plate 1: The Long Gallery, Aston Hall, Birmingham; foreground, a late 16th Century oak table with imported inlaid marble top. (City Museum and Art Gallery, Birmingham: photograph courtesy 'The Connoisseur'.)* **Below,** *Fig. 2: Oak panel depicting scene in Garden of Eden, 16th Century; height 37·5 cm. (Earl of Mount Edgcumbe, Cotehele House, Cornwall: The National Trust.)*

Of the walls of rooms, Harrison recorded that they

> . . . be either hanged with tapestry, arras work, or painted cloths, wherein either divers histories, or herbs, beasts, knots, and such like are stained, or else they are ceiled with oak of our own or wainscot brought hither. . . .[1]

He noticed also that fine possessions were no longer confined to the nobility and gentry, as they had been in the past, but had spread to 'the lowest sort in most places of our south country that have anything at all to take to'.

---

[1] *The word 'ceiled' means that the rooms were panelled either with English oak or with the imported variety. The latter came from the Baltic and was invariably described as 'wainscot', a word of which the origin is disputed.*

Left, *Fig. 3: Mortice-and-tenon joints secured by wooden pegs (dowels).* **Above,** *Fig. 4: Oak 'withdrawing' table, the top extending in length by means of leaves at each end, and the frieze carved with a pattern of rosettes, c. 1600. (Mallett & Son Ltd., London.)*

Certes, in noblemen's houses it is not rare to see abundance of arras, rich hangings of tapestry, silver vessels, and so much other plate as may furnish sundry cupboards to the sum often-times of a thousand or two thousand pounds at the least, whereby the value of this and the rest of their stuff doth grow to be almost inestimable. Likewise, the houses of knights, gentlemen, merchantmen, and some other wealthy citizens, it is not geson to behold generally their great provision of tapestry, Turkey work, pewter, brass, fine linen, and thereto costly cupboards of plate, worth five or six hundred or a thousand pounds to be deemed by estimation.

This state of affairs, Harrison remarked, had in his lifetime 'descended yet lower even unto the inferior artificers and many farmers, who, . . . have, for the most part, learned also to garnish their cupboards with plate, their joined beds with tapestry and silk hangings, and their tables with carpets and fine napery, whereby the wealth of our country (God be praised therefore, and give us grace to employ it well) doth infinitely appear.'

The sudden accumulation of riches by so many people in all ranks of society was a consequence of the adventurous spirit of the age. The voyages of Drake, Hawkins, Raleigh and others resulted in their return from far afield not only with potatoes and tobacco but with precious silver and gold.

The four hundred years that have elapsed between the reigns of the two Queens, Elizabeth I and Elizabeth II, have predictably allowed the disappearance of the majority of furnishings of 16th Century date. To the length of time involved must be added the fact that the total population of England and Wales in the mid-1550's was no more than $2\frac{1}{2}$–3 millions. Although Harrison was greatly impressed by the plenty visible in his day, the overall quantity was quite small. Had it all survived intact there would undoubtedly still be insufficient, to satisfy the demands of present-day collectors.

The major proportion of extant Tudor furniture is made of oak, a timber that was then still plentiful in spite of the inroads made by ship-builders, iron-smelters and

makers of glass into the stock of good trees. Chestnut, yew, pine and others were also employed, perhaps to a greater degree than is now realised. Our knowledge of the woods used is based principally on the remaining furniture, and this leads to the conclusion that practically nothing else was found suitable. References in documents, as well as a few actual examples, show that walnut, while confined to wealthy households, was far from unknown, but lacking the durability of oak it has rarely escaped destruction.

The methods of dealing with the felled tree changed little until modern times, when mechanical power and easily-controlled heat became available. The principal requirement was to store and season the cut planks or they would be unstable, with a certainty of warping and probably the appearance of cracks as the natural moisture dried out. Careful storage for a specific, and usually lengthy, period ensured material on which the craftsman could rely, and which would not develop faults for which his workmanship would be wrongly blamed. The necessity of this

Above, Fig. 5: Oak table, the base with turned legs, scroll brackets, and a frieze carved with a pattern of fluting, c. 1600; length 305 cm. **Above right,** *Fig. 6: Oak 'withdrawing' table, the frieze carved with a pattern of roses and acorns and with winged cherubs' heads at the corners, and the supports in the form of winged human-headed monsters raised on crouching lions, c. 1600; length 241·5 cm. (Both Sotheby's, London.)*

seasoning was well understood by Shakespeare, and also no doubt by his audience, for in *As You Like It* he made Jacques say to Touchstone:

And will you, being a man of your breeding, be married under a bush like a beggar? Get you to church and have a good priest that can tell you what marriage is: this fellow will but join you together as they join wainscot; then one of you will prove a shrunk panel, and like green timber, warp, warp.

In the Middle Ages the trunk was split into planks by means of a wedge driven in at intervals, with a result similar to that of cutting into a round of cheese: a series of pieces each of which is somewhat thicker

at the outer edge than at the inner. By the Sixteenth Century a two-handed saw was in use, and the sawyer and his mate could either cut planks the length and width of the tree or divide the whole into four quarters. These in turn would be sawn, and according to the plan followed the timber produced was more or less likely to distort and split. In the case of oak, the divided quarters gave a more interesting display of grain than did other cuts.

Smoothing was carried out with the adze, a tool occasionally used today, which comprises a flat blade with a curved and sharpened end. Affixed to a handle it is swung carefully so as to hook or chip away the wood to the desired level, so that the finished surface is only approximately flat. The smoothness of the surface relies on the skill of the craftsman, and the undulations remain visible unless further treatment has been given.

Once the wood was ready for furniture-making it came into the hands of either the joiner or the turner. The crafts associated with wood-working were carefully divided, and as early as the year 1400 the joiners had

organised themselves into a separate group. Their speciality was to 'join' their handi-work by means of mortice and tenon, made secure with a dowel. In 1571 the Company of Joiners and Ceilers was incorporated by Royal charter, and all work involving the use of planes and chisels and held together by mortice and tenon was the prerogative of their members.

Turners were limited in their output to what they could make on the lathe. Many of their number were employed in producing drinking-pots, trenchers and other domestic articles, and it is recorded that in 1347 some of them were in trouble for making sub-standard measures for wine and ale. They obtained a charter in 1604, and a list issued four years later shows that they had by then extended their range of goods to include such things as scoops, washing bowls, chairs and wheels.

In London there was supervision to ensure that demarcation between trades was observed. Each craft was supposed to be conducted in isolation, and mixed workshops were frowned upon as likely to spread knowledge of 'secret' processes. In the provinces conditions probably varied from place to place, but on the whole there is little enough information about what ocurred in London and practically none relating to elsewhere in England.

Below, *Fig. 7: Panelled oak armchair with cupboard in base, the back carved with the initials I E S and the date 1574 which was added about 25 years after the chair had been made. Height 139.7 cm. (Victoria & Albert Museum.)* **Opposite,** *Fig. 8: Oak armchair of caquetoire type, the front arcaded and supported on three turned legs and the back inlaid with a geometrical pattern centred on the letter T. Mid-16th Century; height 124.5 cm. (Montacute House, Somerset: The National Trust.)*

There are a number of published, and many unpublished, inventories which contain information about the variety of furniture that was made. The available lists are mostly those of the property of the owners of large houses, and comparatively little can be learned about more commonplace dwellings. By and large, however, the interior of the Tudor house and its occupants are gradually becoming less of a mystery, and some of the misconceptions of earlier research are being corrected.

The mansions of the time varied in plan, but although they boasted a Great Chamber or a Hall it was usual for the big room to be reserved for special occasions, and normally use was made of others more convenient for everyday dining and recreation. In addition, an upper floor was given over to a gallery, measuring anything between 100 and 200 feet in length, although some of them, which have been subsequently destroyed, were even longer. The purpose of the room was to provide space for exercise, during which partakers might admire the views from well-placed windows while they, in turn, were under the gaze of the portraits of their ancestors lining the walls. Elsewhere, there were the kitchen and other offices and, no less important than all the others, the bedrooms.

While the architecture of houses, both as regards their lay-out and their ornamentation, had changed since the beginning of the century, some of the older habits of their occupants persisted. In particular, a chair remained the prerogative of the master, at least on formal occasions, and the normal seating for all other persons was a cushion, a stool or a form. Thus, when the French Ambassador, Monsieur de Maisse, was granted an audience by Queen Elizabeth on 8th December 1597 he recorded that he was led into the Presence Chamber 'where there was a cushion made ready for me'. After a time he was taken into 'a chamber that they call the Privy Chamber, at the head of which was the Queen seated

in a low chair, by herself . . .'. The Ambassador talked to her of various general matters, and then, he noted

> I drew nearer to her chair and began to deal with her in that wherewithall I had been charged; and because I was uncovered, from time to time she signed to me with her hand to be covered, which I did. Soon after she caused a stool to be brought, whereon I sat and began to talk to her'.[1]

The scarcity of chairs in comparison with the number of stools and forms is apparent in inventories, although the heavy construction of most chairs must have ensured that a larger quantity of them have survived than of the once-commonplace alternative seats. The latter were readily portable and doubtless suffered much daily wear-and-

Below, Fig. 9: Oak folding armchair, the 'Glastonbury Armchair'. From Specimens of Ancient Furniture, *by Henry Shaw, 1836.* **Opposite,** *Fig. 10: Oak armchair, the shaped back panel inlaid with a pattern of flowers in a vase inset within carved scrolls and rosettes, and the pierced cresting centred on a man's head above a pair of outstretched wings, c. 1600. (Mallett & Son Ltd.)*

tear. As with much other furniture, the plainer examples will have been less regarded than the ornate, and it is largely the latter that have been preserved. Further, the basic construction of survivors is limited almost exclusively to oak, and others made from less durable woods have long since vanished.

The preceding remarks apply also to tables, of which, with few exceptions, only the more massively-built are extant. In the early 16th Century a number of different types were to be seen, with the majority in the form of a flat top resting on trestles of various patterns. There remain two famous examples at Penshurst, Kent, each of which is 27 feet in length. Not all would have been made on such a large scale, but their clumsiness and plain design would generally have led to rejection by later and more sophisticated generations.

Tables made in the second half of the century were also heavily built, but most were more convenient in size as well as being more decorative in appearance. The larger proportion of them were again in two parts, with the top comprising a number of broad planks held together by cross-members at each end. This rested on a sturdy base of four, six or eight legs linked by a frieze around the upper part and by stretchers below. The design gave the table much greater steadiness than was possible with the trestle, but a disadvantage was that diners seated by the legs found themselves in discomfort. Some of the tables were made adjustable in length, by having at each end a leaf which was arranged to slide out from beneath the top when required. These 'withdraw' or 'withdrawing' tables originated in northern Europe, and were imported from Flanders and elsewhere in addition to being made in England by immigrant and native joiners. The soundness and utility of their design is

---

[1] A Journal of All that was Accomplished by Monsieur de Maisse . . ., *translated from the French by G. B. Harrison and R. A. Jones, The Nonesuch Press, London,* 1931.

Oak stools: **below,** *Fig. 11, of trestle type, the underframe pierced in the shape of a pointed arch. Early 16th Century; height about 51 cm. (Mary Bellis, Hungerford, Berkshire.)* **Right,** *Fig. 12, of joint or 'coffin' type, the frieze carved with oval bosses and the legs turned and fluted. Early 17th Century; width 61 cm. (Sotheby's.)*

The unfortunate term 'coffin stool' was probably applied following the publication of Pepys's Diary *in 1825. On 6th July 1661 he refers to a visit he paid to his father at Brampton, Huntingdonshire, following his uncle Robert's death, where he found "my uncles's corpse in a coffin standing upon joint-stools in the chimney in the hall."*

proved by their remaining in production, unchanged, after more than four hundred years.

The supports of the earlier tables were of plain pattern, relying for ornament on simple mouldings, and in the case of a few specimens on pierced work to lighten the effect without lessening the overall strength. Towards the end of the century, carving and turning were combined to produce a rich appearance, and the two were employed with especial felicity to form the stout 'cup and cover' legs typical of the Elizabethan period (Fig. 1). Although frequently commented upon as a hallmark

Opposite, *Plate 2: Cedarwood armchair, the back surmounted by the crest of the Fauconberg family: a lion rampant with unicorns backed by pennants as supporters, c. 1575. (Temple Newsam House, Yorkshire: Leeds City Art Gallery.)*

Below, *Fig. 13: Carved oak armchair, the seat of canvas held by lacing. (Mary Bellis.)*

of furniture of the time, it was not unknown across the Channel and its use persisted into the first decades of the succeeding century. The legs resemble in outline many of the contemporary silver standing cups, and the likeness to silver models is seen also in the use of gadrooning to ornament friezes.

Not all the tables were carved profusely, but such specimens were more likely to be preserved over the years. A number of plain ones also exist, among them the example in Fig. 5, with unadorned turned legs and a frieze carved with a simple arcaded design. Others are inlaid with geometrical patterns in light and dark woods, and a few bear dates and the initials of their first owners. Always allowing for the possibility that a date has been added subsequently or refers to an event other than the table's making, it can be important in determining the currency of a style and assist in dating others (see Fig. 7).

The most ambitious and rarest of dining tables are of the type illustrated in Fig. 6. It is made of oak, and like the few comparable remaining examples owes much to the engraved designs of Hans Vredeman de Vries and Crispin de Passe, both of whom worked in Antwerp. The table has suffered restoration, as has so much other furniture of the period, but it is surely better that it should be preserved in this way rather than perish completely for lack of attention and appreciation.

The popularity of chess, backgammon and card games is reflected in records of 'playeing tables'. Small in size and of light construction, with very few exceptions they all disappeared long ago. Tables with marble tops, and sometimes also with bases of marble, were to be seen, although whether they were brought home by travellers from Italy or made here is a debatable point. Certainly the extant tops were imported, but it is most probable that wood bases for them were made in England (see Plate 1).

Of chairs, several types were in use during

the second half of the 16th Century. Earlier, many of them had comprised a series of panels framed in uprights and cross-members, the former sometimes carved with simple patterns or with ornament centred on medallions carved with male or female heads. The last was owed to French inspiration, and is sometimes described as 'Romayne'. The furniture of the two countries, England and France, was often not dis-similar in appearance, although the more frequent use of walnut across the Channel enabled their craftsmen to execute carving of a consistently higher standard; the close grain of the wood making it more amenable to the chisel.

The French word *caquetoire* (from *caqueter:* to chatter) was applied in that country to a lightly-made armchair in which ladies were wont to sit and gossip. In England the name has been given to a tall-backed armchair, usually with a wedge-shaped seat and open arms and base, although when they acquired the name is uncertain (Fig. 8).

Another variety has X-shaped side members enabling it to fold for storage. A well-known example is the 'Glastonbury Armchair', named after the first Abbot of Glastonbury, who was executed in 1539 and is supposed to have owned it in his lifetime.

The illustration in Fig. 9 is of an engraving in Henry Shaw's *Specimens of Ancient Furniture*, published in 1836. Shaw wrote of it:

> This chair of simple contrivance is of oak, with carving on it, that marks the early part of the reign of Henry the Eighth. On the upper part of the back, in old English characters, are the words MONACHUS GLASTONIE, and within and without sides of the arms, the inscription JOHANES ARTHURUS.
> Its resemblance to the chair formerly in the priory of Southwick, Hampshire, is evident on the slightest comparison. That religious house was surrendered on the 7th of April, 1539. Instead of the ornamented circle in the back of the Glastonbury chair, is an animal bearing some resemblance to a stag within a square panel, and above two mitres.

The best-known of Elizabethan armchairs are the heavily-built type with turned legs and arm-supports, and carved and inlaid backs. A particularly decorative example is illustrated in Fig. 10, which has the back surmounted by a pierced cresting of scrolls and rosettes centred on a man's head above a pair of outstretched wings. The shaped and arched back panel is inlaid with a vase of formal flowers, which echo the pattern of much of the carving.

2 : Elizabeth I

Chests, Cupboards, Beds

THE low chest dates back to early times, when it was the most useful of a man's possessions. Not only would it serve as a seat, but it contained his worldly goods in safety; protecting them from his fellows as well as from the elements. At a pinch, too, it made a bed, a point made by Oliver

Fig. 14: Oak aumbry, the front pierced with ventilation holes of Gothic pattern. Mid-16th Century; width 104 cm. (Sotheby's.)

Goldsmith who wrote of a later version of it:

> The chest contriv'd a double debt to pay,
> A bed at night, a chest of drawers by day.

The first examples were crudely hollowed tree trunks, and as skills and tools improved the chest's construction likewise advanced. Strength and comparative lightness were achieved by making it with a stout framework enclosing thin panels, the joints being mortice and tenon held firmly by dowels. In due course, a separate variety evolved for travel. The flat surfaces were covered in hide ornamented with round-headed brass nails, and were protected by straps of iron which resisted buffeting and helped to give the whole rigidity.

By the late 16th Century many chests were fitted with a small shallow inner compartment, or till, running from back to front at one end. It was given a hinged cover, which acted also as a support for the lid of the chest itself when the latter was raised. When a chest was the principal, if not only, place of storage, it would be used for clothing, bedding, treasures and much else, and the till conveniently held small items likely to be mislaid if they were not kept separately.

The chest was given at least one strong lock. Some, however, had several as an additional safety measure, and Shakespeare

mentioned 'a jewel in a ten-times-barr'd-up chest'. In churches, for instance, three or more locks are found on chests holding plate and documents of value, so that all who held keys would have to be present (or would have to have surrendered their keys) before the lid could be raised.

The woodwork was ornamented with carving and inlay to suit the taste of the time, but many must have been quite plain and lacking any features that ensured appreciative handling. These have mostly disappeared by now, and the decorated survivors represent no more than a proportion of the variety once in existence. When present, inlaying was often carried out with holly, a white close-grained wood, and bog oak, which becomes stained black throughout after lengthy burial in wet soil.

The design of carving found on chests and other furniture of the period is usually a mixture of the long-established English Gothic and the newly popularised motifs originating in Italy. The former contributed geometrical draughts-board patterns, as well as trellises with cusps at intervals

to relieve the straight lines. The foreign-devised Renaissance innovations were based on natural forms, human, animal and floral, which almost entirely superseded Gothic by the close of the 16th Century. Strange beings, their bodies merging into scrolls, were applied to flat surfaces where-ever there was space to accommodate them, while full-length personages depicted Biblical events or mythological scenes, or were posed with their attributes to represent the Seasons. The jagged leaf of the acanthus, beloved of ancient Greece, appeared frequently, and all kinds of raised bosses and studs were carved on friezes and elsewhere. Negotiating a well-furnished room might well have demanded wearing the voluminous padded clothing of the time, or have resulted in much laceration of the unwary.

The oval boss or cabochon was sometimes converted into a gadroon: a series of finger-like projections arranged on the angle, and sometimes found decorating the frieze of a table. Another much-used motif was the rosette, of which a series was carved between continuous interlinked shallow channels running from end to end of a surface. It was common for panels to be given arched tops, as in Fig. 15, when the shaped portion would be boldly carved to emphasize its contour.

One particularly ornate type of chest is known as a 'Nonsuch Chest'. In each instance, the front and sides are inlaid with representations of pinnacled buildings somewhat resembling the Palace of that name, which once stood near Cheam, Surrey. It was built for Henry VIII and

demolished in 1670, but its appearance is recorded in a drawing made in 1568 which was published in an engraving in 1582 (see Fig. 18 and Plate 3). The distinctive inlaying, which is much more complex than that usually seen on pieces made in England at the date, is similar to that found on contemporaneous German furniture. The engravings of Nonsuch, as well as the fame of the palace, would have circulated far and wide, and it is not improbable that it inspired craftsmen abroad. There were, however, immigrant workers from many lands pursuing their trades in London, including some Germans settled in Southwark, and they may have been responsible for some of the chests. There is no evidence that the architectural fancies portrayed on

the chests were intended to represent Nonsuch, and they would appear to have acquired their popular name long after they were made.

A living-room generally contained a cupboard of some kind for storing food, usually with its front and sides pierced to allow ventilation. Known as an aumbry or almery it was used throughout the 16th Century. Thomas Tusser, in his book *Five Hundred Points of Good Husbandry*, published in 1573, noted:

> Some slovens from sleeping, no sooner be up,
> But hand is in aumbrie, and nose in the cup.[1]

The name seems to have originated in the French *armoire:* a cupboard, which was duly anglicised. At some periods it was used for storing books, and at others the

[1] *Quoted by John Gloag in* A Short Dictionary of Furniture.

Left, *Fig. 16: Sturdy oak chest, the curved lid with shaped ends pivoting on wood pegs. 15th Century; width 124·5 cm. (Montacute House, Somerset).* **Below,** *Fig. 17: Oak chest of boarded type (cf. the more usual framed panels), the front carved with tracery and formal patterns bordered by crosshatching. Mid-16th Century; width 134·5 cm. (Temple Newsam House, Yorkshire.)*

Above, *Fig. 18: Nonsuch Palace, Cheam, Surrey, built for Henry VIII and demolished in 1670. Engraved by Höfnagel for Georg Braun's* Urbium Praecipuarium Mundi Theatrum Quintum, *published in 1582.* (Mansell Collection.)

Opposite, *Fig. 19: Oak court cupboard with turned supports between the shelves and the ends panelled. Late 16th Century; width 129·5 cm. (Sotheby's.)*

left-overs from a meal were temporarily put aside in it prior to be given away as alms by an almoner: alms, almoner and almery obviously sharing a common origin. In churches, a cupboard of similar appearance stood beside the altar to contain the chalice and other altar furnishings when not in use.

Extant examples dating from the reigns of the Tudors are very few in number. With the improved planning of houses, food would have had no permanent place in the living quarters, and would have been kept in the kitchen or pantry before and after a meal. Plainer cupboards employed for the same purpose would have been found in the houses and cottages of most of the populace, but being of utilitarian pattern and suffering much wear and tear would

have been thrown aside from time to time and replaced.

Of greater importance than the aumbry, although less rare, is the piece of furniture referred to in the past as a Court Cupboard. At one time there existed confusion as to the precise meaning of the term, but the late R. W. Symonds produced evidence about it which has been widely accepted.[1] He found in a book entitled *Perspective Practical*, published in 1672, an engraving of two 'Court cup-boards' which shows two sets of open shelves used for displaying plate and to assist those serving a meal. In both rôles it was duly supplanted by the side table and the sideboard. The generic word 'cupboard' (literally meaning a board for cups) was used for other varieties, all having pairs of doors to enclose the upper stage or both lower and upper parts.

Many of the open court cupboards exhibit features similar to those already discussed in connexion with tables of the time. The bulbous legs of the latter re-appear as shelf supports, gadroons and rosettes are equally

---

[1] *'The "Dyning Parlour" and its Furniture', by R. W. Symonds, in* The Connoisseur, *January 1944.*

popular as carved motifs, and oak is the favoured timber for construction. A number of examples were of walnut and a few survive, but mention of others in inventories proves that they were once less scarce than they are today.

Although simple inlay of floral and geometrical patterns was used, the principal ornament was carved. Exceptional specimens have their supports in the shape of heraldic beasts, and occasionally human figures, full- or half-length performed the

same function. From contact with floors, which may often have been damp, the lowest platform of a court cupboard has sometimes rotted and been replaced at a later date, therefore this part should always be examined with extra attention.

Where doors are present in a cupboard, they are found to bear decoration of conventional pattern, with carving cut below the surface and only occasionally projecting above it. Uprights between doors are left plain except for simple mouldings, shallow carving, or applied lengths of projecting carving. These last take various forms, among the most attractive being examples based on the designs of de Vries and others (Fig. 21).

Left, Fig. 20: Oak court cupboard, the supports turned and carved and the shelves carved with gadroons and fluting, c. 1600; width about 137 cm. (Mallett & Son Ltd.)
Below, *Fig. 21: Designs for grotesque pilasters, by Jan Vredeman de Vries, 1527–1604?*

L AST but not least, consideration must be given to the largest, and usually the most splendid, piece of furniture in a Tudor house: the bed. In the past the importance of the bed was in the materials with which it was hung, the wooden structure being a secondary consideration. The bedstead formed a room within a room, the occupant

being completely insulated from cold air and draughts to such a degree that suffocation might be thought to have been a commonplace. In fact it was not, but one exhibitor at the 1851 Great Exhibition had obviously given the matter due consideration and displayed a four-poster with ventilating tubes leading through the top. It may be recalled that William Shakespeare bequeathed to his wife his 'second-best' bed. By this he referred to the quality of its hangings rather than to the comfort and appearance of the piece of furniture.

Below, *Fig. 22: Carved oak bedstead, the tester restored. Mid-16th Century; width 183 cm. (Sotheby's.)* **Right,** *Fig. 23: Oak bedstead with turned and carved end supports and panelled head and tester. Late 16th Century. (Mallett & Son Ltd.)*

By the mid-16th Century, although cur-
tains and valances continued to be used, the
head, posts and tester were carved instead
of being left plain. An example is illustrated in Fig. 22, although in this instance the
tester is a restoration. The bed was at one
time in the possession of the Reverend
William Allen, of Lovely Hall, near Black-
burn, and was illustrated by Henry Shaw
in his *Specimens of Ancient Furniture,*
published in 1836. Shaw depicted it
showing the upper portion engraved only
lightly, and wrote:

> This interesting example, which un-
> fortunately has lost its true cornice,
> no doubt highly enriched, was observed
> by Mr Allen in the course of his pro-
> fessional duties, in administering to a
> dying parishioner the last consolation
> of religion, and purchased by him after
> the decease of the sick person from his
> heir.

Thereafter the bed vanished from record
until sometime in the present century.

The most renowned of Tudor beds is the
Great Bed of Ware, which was seen and
noted by a traveller in 1596, probably soon
after it had been made. After many subse-
quent references by those who saw and
were amazed by it, it eventually found a
worthy home in the Victoria and Albert
Museum. The bed, in which it was once
reported that six Londoners and their
wives had spent a night, measures 10 ft.
8½ inches in width, but this was not exceptional at the date of its making. Paul
Hentzner, a German visitor to England in
1578, saw at Windsor

> a chamber in which are the royal beds
> of Henry VII. and his queen, of Edward
> VI., of Henry VIII., and of Anne
> Bullen (Boleyn), all of them eleven

feet square, and covered with quilts
shining with gold and silver; queen
Elizabeth's bed, with curious coverings
of embroidery, but not quite so long or
large as the others. . . .

The bed illustrated in Fig. 23 embodies
many of the features of the Great Bed and
others contemporary with it. The profusion
of carving is especially typical, and the
posts, each with two large bulbous turnings, echo the legs of tables and the supports
of Court cupboards. The tester, like the
headboard, is divided into panels, carved
and inlaid, set into patterned mouldings
and was, possibly, once embellished with
paint and gold leaf.

Hentzner recorded also the rich appearance of the queen's bed at Whitehall Palace,
which was, he said

> ingeniously composed of woods of
> different colours, with quilts of silk,
> velvet, gold, silver, and embroidery.

While, at the Tower of London,

> we were obliged to quit our swords at
> the gate, and deliver them to the guard.
> When we were introduced, we were
> shown above a hundred pieces of arras[1]
> belonging to the crown, made of gold,
> silver, and silk; several saddles covered
> with velvet of different colours; an
> immense quantity of bed-furniture,
> such as canopies, and the like, some of
> them most richly ornamented with
> pearl. . . .

Another Tudor bed, shown in Fig. 24,
has a number of points of resemblance to
the example in Fig. 23. Although the
maker has been less lavish with timber for
the turned sections of the posts, he has
compensated by providing massive square
bases for each of them. The side members
clearly show the holes through which were
threaded rope to support the mattresses;

---

[1] *Arras: wall-hangings; the name derived from the
Flemish (now French) town whence many were imported.*

Below, *Fig. 25: Bedstead 'judiciously compiled' from a late 16th Century table and from fragments of carving of various dates. Width 183 cm.*

Right, *Plate 4; Court cupboard of walnut inlaid with holly and bog oak, the friezes fitted with drawers. Circa 1590; width 127 cm. (Victoria and Albert Museum.)*

additional rope ran from end to end to provide an unyielding base. According to the wealth of the sleeper, and the standard of comfort demanded, he lay on feathers, combed-out wool, flock or straw, and John Evelyn, writing in 1664, recommended beech leaves 'gathered about the fall, and somewhat before they are frostbitten'.

Bedsteads were strongly built and frequently lasted for several generations of a family. Many Elizabethan examples remained in their original places well into the 19th Century and, in a few instances, still later. During the Tudor revival of the 1830's they came in for their share of attention, and not a few came on the market; gladly purchased by antique-collectors of the day, and as gladly sold by those who wanted more up-to-date furnishings.

Some of the old beds, or fragments of them, received attention from both amateurs and professionals, who took pains to repair them and at the same time 'improved' them so that they more readily found buyers. This was common practice and not confined to bedsteads, as was made clear by J. C. Loudon when he wrote the following words in 1829:[1]

> The exterior of . . . chests or wardrobes might be rendered curious, and highly interesting, though we do not say in correct or architectural taste, by covering them with the Elizabethan, Dutch, Louis XIV., or Francis I. ornaments, which are now to be purchased in abundance, either at home or abroad. We have already referred to Nixon and Son [with premises in Great Portland Street], for the two latter kinds of furniture; and we may here observe that Wilkinson of Oxford Street, and Hanson of John Street, have extensive collections of Elizabethan and Dutch furniture and carvings, from which a judicious compiler of exteriors might clothe skeleton frames, so as to produce objects of curiosity and interest, at a very trifling expense. Kensett of Mortimer Street has also some curious specimens of both Elizabethan and more ancient furniture.

From the number of surviving examples of their workmanship, there was no shortage of 'judicious compilers of exteriors' from that date onwards. Not only did they add details to taste but, worse still, they took up their chisels and added whatever carving they thought necessary; while glued and nailed additions are removable, carved work remains forever. All kinds of furniture suffered, and the wreckers pursued their activities in company with others who eagerly embossed good plain silver or grangerised books. It is odd that so many people have during the past 150 years considered themselves competent to improve on the past, while others have aided and abetted them by buying their handiwork.

A good example of the workmanship of an anonymous 'improver' is the bed illustrated in Fig. 25. It is obvious that the base has been constructed from part of an Elizabethan table, with a gadrooned frieze and good turned and carved legs. The extraordinary animals *sejant* are much later in date, while the posts carved with vine leaves and grapes were probably the work of a 17th-Century craftsman. The whole is a remarkable mixture of styles, and as it is known to have been in existence at least since 1840, it probably saw the light of day in its present unsightly form soon after Loudon wrote the words quoted above.

---

[1] *In his* Encyclopædia of Cottage, Farm and Villa Architecture and Furniture.

3 : James I

THE difficulty of describing accurately the furniture of a past period increases with the interval of time. Examples will have survived for a number of reasons so that they may not be truly representative

Fig. 26: 'Farthingale' chair on walnut supports, the seat and back covered in woollen fabric with applied embroidery of which much is now missing. First quarter of the 17th Century; height 91·5 cm. (Victoria and Albert Museum.)

articles, and numerous pieces, once commonplace and typical of a home of the time, have possibly disappeared for ever. Portrait paintings are often reliable guides, but fashion did not insist that sitters should invariably be posed inside their houses and surrounded by their possessions. Had this been the case, then the work of future furniture historians would have been made immensely easier.

The contemporaneous written word, where it has been preserved, can be helpful, but has to be read with the proviso that meanings change, like fashions in clothing, and it is often hard to determine what is described but not pictured. The most helpful of all are documents and inventories, but these varied in comprehensiveness as much in the past as they do today. Some of them were fairly detailed and obviously accurate, but many of their compilers would seem to have been content with supplying a minimum of description which now has only slight value. We do not know what may have been the custom of past times in this matter, and it is unclear whether it was taken for granted that what a valuer considered unimportant might be omitted from his list. Certainly, many would seem to have taken it upon themselves to do so, as their inventories are noticeably brief. Quite a number of such documents dating from the 16th and 17th Centuries suggest that rooms were almost

bare except for the basic chair, table and cupboard; a picture that is not compatible with other records of life in those days.

Raph. Byrd and his two colleagues, who took and signed an inventory of the possessions of the late Lady Anne Mohun in 1608, seem to have been particularly conscientious in their work. Lady Mohun was the second wife and widow of Sir William Mohun, and lived at Hall, a mansion situated above the river opposite Fowey, in Cornwall. Writing in 1603, Richard Carew, the historian of the county, described her as 'a Lady, gracing her dignitie, with her vertue, and no lesse expressing, then professing religion'. The furnishing of the dining room of the house is probably comparable with that of others in other parts of England, and the carefully-compiled list, with its phonetic spelling, merits printing:[1]

In the dineing chamber

One green carpett with silke fring	4. 0. 0.
one other green carpett old	10. 0.
one canopie chaier with silke courtains and fring	3. 0. 0.
one side cubbord	13. 4.
one smale squar table	10. 0.
one Turkey carpett with arms imbrothered	2. 0. 0.
twoe green cloth cubbord cloaths	6. 0.
a paier of virginalls	1. 6. 8.
twelve cushions of Irish stitch	1. 4. 0.
one chaier of green cloth oversett with flowers	13. 4.
one blewe cloath chaier with silke fring	10. 0.
one childs chaier	2. 0.
one chaier of redd and yellow stript stuffe	4. 0.
twoe old ioyne stooles	2. 0.
three ioyn stooles covered with needle worke	9. 0.
three ioyn stooles of Turkey worke	5. 0.
sixe stooles of green cloath fringed	15. 0.
fower lowe Flemishe chaiers	8. 0.
one lowe chaier covered with needle worke	2. 0.
a paier of tonngs, a fier pane and billowes old	6.
five pictuers	1. 0. 0.
fower peecs of arras	4. 0. 0.
twoe lowe stooles of stuffe	.. 5. 0.
twoe paier of tables and one form	8. 8.

[1] *The original is in the Cornwall County Record Office, Truro.*

Opposite, *Plate 5: Oak bedstead, the headboard carved with the coats of arms of James I of England and Frederick V, Elector Palatine of the Rhine, and the badge of Henry, Prince of Wales. Early 17th Century; width 188 cm. (Montacute House, Somerset; The National Trust.)*

Below, *Fig. 27: Armchair and footstool of beech-wood upholstered in velvet studded with brass-headed nails, formerly in the possession of William Juxon, Archbishop of Canterbury (1582–1663), who attended Charles I on the scaffold. Second quarter of the 17th Century; height 127 cm. (Victoria and Albert Museum.)*

From the above, it is clear that in every instance the covering on a piece of furniture constituted its value, and whereas 'twoe old ioyne stooles' were worth no more than 2s., a single joint stool covered in needlework was listed at three times the

amount. An entry 'In the Wardrobe' provides evidence that the latter was executed by Lady Mohun, or at anyrate by someone in the house:

one fram for an imbrotherer and a Turkey workeframe   6. 8.

The mention of a canopy chair 'with silke courtains and fring' makes intriguing reading, and may be compared with an equally unusual example known to have

Left, Fig. 28: Child's chair of oak, the supports partly turned and the back carved with conventional patterns. Early 17th Century; height about 102 cm. Below, Fig. 29: Child's chair of carved oak. Mid-17th Century; height about 61 cm. (Both Mary Bellis.)

Below, *Fig. 30: Child's chair of oak, the back panelled and carved with floral patterns. Mid-17th Century; height about 102 cm. (Mary Bellis.)*

Opposite, *Fig. 31: Oak folding-top table with a carved frieze and turned supports. Mid-17th Century; width 71 cm. (Sotheby's.)*

been in the possession of Queen Elizabeth early in her reign. It was described as

> one great stool of wallnutre with one large pillow covered with cloth of gold and ffrenged with silk and gold, with one staie for the back of the Queen covered with cloth of gold with staies, springes, and staples of iron to set the same higher and lower with a pillow of down.

No doubt both chairs were designed to defeat draughts and give the users greater comfort than normal.

Turkey work, which was extremely popular at the time and of which examples survive, was a type of coarse needlework made in imitation of carpets imported from Turkey and elsewhere in the Middle East. It was employed occasionally for making actual carpets, but is usually described as covering the seats of stools and chairs and for the backs of the latter. Like other kinds of fabric, Turkey work carpets were often used on the tops of tables and cabinets, and a few Tudor and Stuart paintings show them thus employed.

The 'twelve cushions of Irish stitch' were worked in a particular type of embroidery which received a brief mention from the pen of John Taylor, a waterman on the river Thames and known as the 'Water Poet', who wrote in 1634:

> For Tent-worke, Raisd-worke Laid-worke, Frost-worke, Net-worke
> Most curious Purles, or rare Italian Cutworke,
> Fine Ferne-stitch, Finny-stitch, New-stitch and Chain-stitch,
> Braue Bred-stitch, Fisher-stitch, Irish-stitch, and Queene-stitch. . . .
> All these are good and these we must allow
> And these are everywhere in practise now.[1]

The chairs described as Flemish may have been imported from Flanders, or were perhaps made in England by immigrant

---

[1] *See Margaret H. Swain,* Historical Needlework, *1970, pages 117-18 for a discussion of Irish stitch and others.*

workers or possibly by Englishmen following a Continental pattern. Finally, it may be noticed that most of Lady Mohun's furniture was upholstered, suggesting that even at a distance of over 200 miles from the capital the standard of comfort was a high one. Confirmation is given to the words of William Harrison, which had been written thirty or forty years before:

> The furniture of our houses also exceedeth, and is grown in manner even to passing delicacy. . . .

QUEEN ELIZABETH died in 1602, and was succeeded on the throne by the first member of the House of Stuart, James I. Son of Mary, Queen of Scots, he had reigned as James VI of Scotland since 1567, and his assumption of the crown of England united the two countries. Whatever else was

Left, *Fig. 32: Oak hanging food cupboard with carved and inlaid ornament. Early 17th Century; width about 61 cm. (Mary Bellis.)* **Below,** *Fig. 33: Oak folding-top table, the ornament carved and flanked by applied split turnings. First half of 17th Century; width 96·5 cm. (Mallett & Son Ltd.)*

Above, *Fig. 34: Oak court cupboard, the fronts of the shelves carved with oval bosses and flanked by foliate trusses, the slender turned columns reeded. Early 17th Century; width 119·5 cm. (Sotheby's.)*
Opposite, *Fig. 35: Oak cupboard with panelled doors, the upper frieze carved with rosettes and supported by reeded turned members with Ionic capitals. First half of 17th Century; width 129·5 cm. (Mary Bellis.)*

achieved by this event, the artistic effect was not noticeable. Unlike other foreign arrivals in London, James brought with him no detectable aesthetic influences from north of the Border, so it will be seen that there was little change to be observed between furniture made at the beginning of his reign and the end of it.

On the whole his tenancy of the throne was a quiet one, in which there was a steady pressure directed by the Puritans against all forms of display. In particular, the target for their venom was the stage, and many writers spent their time pouring scorn on players, playwrights and the public who patronised them. This had been occurring during the last quarter of the 16th Century when, among others, Phillip Stubbes made a swingeing attack on the amusements of the time. In his *Anatomie of Abuses*, which was published in 1583, he wrote at length and in colourful language of the stage, and included the following passage:

> Doo these Mockers and Flowters of his Maiesty, these dissembling Hipocrites, and flattering Gnatoes, think to escape vnpunished? beware, therfor, you masking Players, you painted sepulchres, you doble dealing ambodexters, be warned betimes, and, lik good computistes, cast your accompts before, what wil be the reward therof in the end, least God destroy you in his wrath: abuse God no more, corrupt his people no longer with your dregges, and intermingle not his blessed word with such prophane vanities.

The argument was not at all one-sided, with pamphlets appearing in a steady flow. The writer Thomas Nashe put the argument in favour in these words, and others used similar plausible reasoning:

> For whereas the after-noone beeing the idlest time of the day; wherein men that are their owne masters (as Gentlemen of the Court, the Innes of the Courte, and the number of Captaines and Souldiers about London) do wholy bestow themselues vpon pleasure, and that pleasure they deuide (howe vertuously it skils not) either into gameing, following of harlots, drinking, or seeing a Playe: is it not then better (since of foure extreames all the world cannot keepe them but they will choose one) that they should betake them to the least, which is Playes?[1]

By 1600, the anti-stage lobby had got as far as inducing the Privy Council to ban all but two of the theatres in the London area, but the local authorities concerned ignored the injunction and the dispute continued while the players went their way as before.

---

[1] *From* Pierce Penilesse his Supplication to the Diuell, *1592. For contemporary records of the controversy see E. K. Chambers,* The Elizabethan Stage, *4 vols., Oxford, 1923, vol. iv, pp. 184-345.*

Fig. 36: Oak court cupboard, the shelf fronts shaped and carved with rosettes and the supports partly carved with scales. Early 17th Century; width 106·8 cm. (Mallett & Son Ltd.)

Despite the clamour of the opposition, or perhaps because of it, drama flourished, and it was between 1600 and 1616 that most of William Shakespeare's plays were written and first performed. The first of them to be printed did not appear until 1597, when *Richard II* was issued in quarto form without a mention of the author's name, but most of the plays remained unread by the public until publication of the First Folio in 1623.

Shakespeare's plays contain a number of references to homes of his time, and there are some interesting mentions of furniture. Thus, in *Romeo and Juliet* the servants hurry to clear the dining hall so that a masque can take place, and one of them says:

> Away with the joint-stools, remove the court-cupboard, look to the plate. . . .

In other words, remove the silverware from the shelves of the court cupboard, and take away the latter as well as the joint stools. The play was written in 1591 or 1592, and

such furniture must have been in use at the time or the audience would not have understood the meaning of the words.

He also mentions day beds, which were used for casual resting although presumably only in wealthy homes. Such articles presumably had wood frames and ends, but their principal feature would have been one or more well-stuffed cushions. An example, attributed to *circa* 1600, is illustrated in the *Dictionary of English Furniture* (1954 edition, vol. ii, page 135). It is of oak, the outwards-sloping ends panelled and painted with arabesques and with coats of arms, and although the trimmed valances are not original, the long cushion still bears the rose-coloured damask with which it was first covered.

While drama flourished successfully, the minor art of interior decoration and furniture design produced little that had not been seen before, and concentrated on reducing the ostentation and extravagance that had marked much Tudor work. The most noticeable alteration was the gradual replacement of the carved bulbous support by a plain turned member of straight or slightly curved profile. Chairs certainly became more commonplace than they had been, and the custom of reserving them solely for important persons died out.

The joint stool continued to be made much as before, but also acquired a back and became a single chair. Its introduction took place prior to the turn of the century, although few surviving examples pre-date 1600. It has been presumed that it was 'devised in order that the huge-hipped farthingale might be displayed to its full extent when its wearer was seated'. There is no proof that this was the case, although such chairs have been called 'farthingale chairs' since some unknown date. That the costume caused difficulty is proved by the fact that an order was issued in 1613 denying admittance to Court masques of ladies wearing farthingales, because so arrayed they were difficult or impossible to seat. It is, perhaps, doubtful if any chair could have accommodated Anne of Denmark Queen of James I, when, in 1617, a contemporary described the costume she wore as being of 'pink and gold, with so expansive a farthingale that I do not exaggerate when I say that it was four feet wide at the hips'. Chairs of the type have survived on a reduced scale and, remarkably little altered in appearance from those of the early 1600's. 20th-Century versions are used in Westminster Abbey on the occasion of Coronations.

Less scarce than single chairs, early 17th-Century armchairs exist in various forms. Most of them are similar to those of Tudor date, with wooden seats, turned supports and tall backs. A few examples

that can be dated with accuracy show that carving was more popular than inlay as ornament, but they have not survived in sufficient numbers for firm conclusions to be drawn.

The X-frame type continued to be made, and Horace Walpole wrote of them, 'cross-legged and . . . in their original coverings, all with their attendant stools squatting beside them', after he had visited Knole Park, Sevenoaks. Many of them remain in the mansion, which is now in the care of the National Trust. The frames of the chairs are of beech-wood, a timber normally prone to attack by woodworm, but in these examples protection against their ravages has been fortuitously given by the fabric glued and nailed to the legs, arms and uprights of the backs.

A chair of similar appearance to the preceding specimens was once the property of William Juxon, Archbishop of Canterbury, who attended Charles I on the

Fig. 37: Panelled and carved oak chest.
First quarter of 17th Century; width
132 cm. (Mary Bellis.)

Left, *Fig. 38: Panelled oak chest carved with stylised floral patterns. Early 17th Century; width 127·5 cm. (Montacute House, Somerset.)*

Right, *Plate 6: Oak armchair, the back panelled and carved centrally with a floral design within an arch. The feet have been restored. Early 17th Century. (Montacute House, Somerset.)*

scaffold in 1649. The chair, together with a stool, was acquired by the Victoria and Albert Museum in 1928, and is described as 'covered with discoloured velvet, originally crimson'. Earlier, in 1794, a writer in the *Gentleman's Magazine* gave the colour as a purple, and added:

> I was told they [the chair and stool] were used on the scaffold at the horrid execution, and that his Majesty kneeled on the stool when he received the fatal stroke; and the spots of blood yet remaining on the velvet seem to corroborate the story.

The engraving of the chair and stool printed in the *Magazine* show such distortions of the actual articles, that it may be wondered whether artist or writer ever saw the originals. The story given above and another that the King sat in the chair during his trial in Westminster Hall, remain unproven, but the connexion with the Archbishop is not questioned (Fig. 27).

While there are few extant examples of small pieces of furniture made before 1600, rather more have survived from after that year. The larger an article the more durable it is, and the lightweight portable pieces are invariably the first to suffer from daily usage, accident, or from strokes of the axe when firewood is desperately required. As in other periods, precise dating is often difficult unless a year is carved on a piece

and it can be substantiated. London styles set the standard for the remainder of the country, but took time before they percolated to the outer regions and a decade or two might elapse between a City introduction and its provincial acceptance. No doubt the London craftsmen would have been the most skilful and made the more sophisticated use of currently fashionable motifs, but time has blurred many of the subtle distinctions once readily apparent.

While the large dining table continued to be made in a modified form, differing from Tudor ones mostly as regards the diameter and lack of carving of the legs, smaller tables came into increasing use. Whereas knowledge of their existence in Tudor times relies largely on mentions in documents, a fair number of 17th-Century examples are extant. One type, which is fitted with a cupboard, is sometimes referred to as a Credence table; taking its name from the Latin (*credere:* to believe) as some of them were used in churches to contain the reserved sacrament. As with much 17th-Century silverware, it is often impossible to distinguish between pieces made for ecclesiastical use and those intended for the home, and most of the tables doubtless began their service in dining rooms.

Another variety of table, lacking any cupboard but with a hinged top opening to be

supported by a swinging leg, the first appearance of the ever-popular gate-leg, is also known as a Credence table. In this instance the name is explained by its use before meals, when a servant would stand by it to sample the food to be served. Paul Hentzner described the ceremony followed at Court, where, after some preliminary plate cleaning with bread and salt:

> the yeomen of the guards entered, bareheaded, clothed in scarlet, with a golden rose upon their backs, bringing in at each turn a course of twenty-four dishes, served in plate, most of it gilt; these dishes were received by a gentleman in the same order they were brought, and placed upon the table, while the lady-taster gave to each of the guard a mouthful to eat, of the particular dish he had brought for fear of poison.

Whether the so-called Credence tables played any part in the ritual, either at Court or in less exalted circumstances, is open to doubt.

The surviving tables are only rarely to be found in their original state. Where folding tops are present, these have often been renewed, wholly or partially, especially the hinged section, while feet have suffered from contact with damp floors and the rotted parts have been renewed. A table with a simple fixed top has sometimes had a further portion added and a gate has been provided to support it, so making a more useful article. Many of these alterations were made forty or more years ago, and the inexperienced may find them very difficult to detect.

Fig. 39: Oak chest, the front inset with ten panels carved with an arched design and the framework with lunettes and rosettes. First quarter of 17th Century; width about 168 cm. (Mary Bellis.)

4 : Charles I

CHARLES I, second son of James I, succeeded to the throne in March 1625. Two months previously he had been married by proxy to the fifteen-year-old Henrietta Maria, daughter of the French King, Henri

Fig. 40: Turned or 'thrown' armchair. 17th Century; height 95 cm. (Montacute House, Somerset; The National Trust.)

IV and Marie de Medicis. Before then, in 1623, Charles, when Prince of Wales, had undertaken a journey to Spain in an attempt to win the affections of the Infanta Maria. He went there in company with the Duke of Buckingham, and not only did he find his prospective bride averse to his proposal, but her father, Philip III, showed no interest in suggested plans to assist Charles's brother-in-law, Frederick of Bohemia, in regaining his throne. From this he had been driven only four days after his coronation and, dying at the age of 36, left a widow who survived him for thirty years; a lady of considerable charm who earned the title of 'Queen of Hearts', but is often referred to as the 'Winter Queen'.

The intrigue and counter-intrigue during Charles's stay in Madrid expedited his return to England. One result of the visit, however fruitless it may have been in other aspects, was that it gave the future King an opportunity of seeing some of the riches of the Habsburgs. The numerous portraits by Titian, Rubens and Velasquez must have introduced him to the existence of accomplished styles of painting scarcely known in his own country. In the words of E. K. Waterhouse, 'he saw for the first time what eloquence of authoritative persuasion could reside in a royal image'.[1]

In due time, in 1632, seven years after he had ascended the throne, the King welcomed from abroad Anthony van Dyck,

---

[1]Painting in Britain, 1530-1790, *1953, p. 36.*

who had been in England previously for a brief stay. He was speedily appointed 'principalle Paynter in ordinary to their Majesties', received the honour of knighthood, and recorded brilliantly the likenesses of many of his distinguished contemporaries.

It was insufficient for Charles to emulate the King of Spain by lining the walls of his palaces with portraits of his family, his friends and himself. He set about forming a collection to compare with what he had seen on his travels, and with those elsewhere of which he had read reports. While still a youth of 12, he had inherited the pictures belonging to his elder brother, Henry, who had died suddenly when only eighteen years of age. They formed a nucleus to which Charles added, and duly built up to make a collection worthy of a royal house.

The King showed little interest in the arts other than painting, and his acquisition of Old Masters has caused posterity to place his judgement of them far above his political wisdom. His lack of the latter quality, so essential for the occupant of a throne, led to his beheading and the regrettable dispersal of his collection to settle the debts that survived him.

The King was the centre of a group of Englishmen who were eagerly forming collections of works of art; an innovation in modern Europe, in which the first important participant was Rudolph II, a scholarly Habsburg and a relative of Philip of Spain. The foremost among the Englishmen was Thomas Howard, second Earl of Arundel, the remainder of whose legendary accumulation of ancient marbles is now in the Asmolean Museum, Oxford. Among other members of the nobility similarly interested was the Duke of Buckingham, who suddenly began to collect Italian paintings and amassed a great quantity of them during the few years between 1620 and 1628, when he died. The latter's adviser was a Netherlands immigrant, Sir Balthazar Gerbier,

who had some skill as a miniature-painter and doubtful talent as a diplomatist, but was certainly responsible for bringing to England the work of a large number of hitherto unknown artists.

Opposite, Plate 7: Oak table with a shaped frieze and turned supports. Early 17th Century; width 80·7 cm. (Montacute House, Somerset.)

Below, Fig. 41: Oak chair-table decorated with applied ornament. Mid-17th Century; height 134·7 cm. (Victoria and Albert Museum: Photograph, Mary Bellis.)

Gerbier was not alone in importing the rich and rare, and the supply was swelled noticeably by the contributions of Sir Henry Wotton and Sir Dudley Carleton, of whom the first-named was Ambassador at Venice and the second served in the same capacity both there and at The Hague. In addition, wealthy people were travelling far and wide, returning with treasures for the embellishment of their homes and, incidentally and unwittingly, the enrichment of future generations of their families.

While many people concentrated their attention on oil-paintings, there can be no doubt that they also saw and bought other objects including furniture. Thus, an inventory of the contents of Tart Hall, St. James's, noting the possessions of Lady Arundel, included:

In the little closett in the West side of ye Drawing Room: a large cubberd fashioned Indian chest; an Indian chest; a little black Indian table; an Indian standish.
In the Parlour chamber: a large cubberd fashioned Indian cabinett, a lowe Indian table with a little Indian chest.

The list was compiled in 1641, and the use of the term 'Indian' at that date, and much later, often means that the articles were brought to the west in ships of the East

Below, *Fig. 42: The chair-table in Fig. 41, shown in the form of a table. Like many combination objects, these pieces are inferior in both respects.*

Fig. 43: Oak settle, the tall back inset with fifteen carved panels. 17th Century; height 162·5 cm. (Mary Bellis.)

India Company, and they did not necessarily originate in that country.

The Oriental pieces at Tart Hall may have been imported direct to London, or they may have reached there by way of Rotterdam and the Dutch East India Company. Alternatively, the Earl of Arundel may have bought them somewhere in Europe during his many journeyings. His taste embraced not only the Far East, and the house contained furniture from nearer at hand, such as:

*Below, Fig. 44: Armchair of painted and gilt pinewood, probably designed by Francis Cleyn (1582–1658) in about 1625. Height 110·5 cm. **Opposite,** Fig. 45: Oak folding-top table with gate leg, the frieze shaped and carved with leaf patterns. Second quarter of the 17th Century; width about 91·5 cm. (Mallett & Son Ltd.)*

A French drawing table of walnut tree with a leather carpet thereon.
Sixe Italian chayres of wood carved.
A little ebony square table inlayde with Torteaux shels.
A large Trunke of Mother of Pearle with two drawers.
Nyne great Italian chayres of walnut tree with armes, the seats and backs covered with red leather sett with brass nails gilt.[1]

Style as well as comfort were demanded by Lady Compton, who, a little earlier, stated her furnishing requirements firmly and with clarity. She wrote:

I will have all my houses furnished, and all my lodging chambers to be suited with all such furniture as is fit; as beds, stools, chairs, suitable cushions, carpets, silver warming pans, cupboards of plate, fair hangings, and such like. So for my drawing chambers in all houses I will have them delicately furnished both with couch, canopy, glass, carpet, chairs, cushions, and all things therunto belonging.[2]

On the other hand, a house in the country, some 250 miles from the capital, might be expected to have less luxurious and less up-to-date contents than one in or near London, especially if the owner was not outstandingly wealthy. The hitherto unpublished inventory of the contents of Roskrow, near Falmouth, Cornwall, proves this to have been the case. It details the property of Samuel Pendarves, was dated 30th September 1643, and including 'goods and trifells omitted' came to a total sum of £960. The principal rooms were the hall

[1] *The Tart Hall inventory was printed in* The Burlington Magazine, *November 1911, and January and March 1912.*

[2] *G. Goodman,* The Court of King James I, *quoted by M. Jourdain,* English Decoration and Furniture of the Early Renaissance, *1924.*

and parlour, of which the contents were as follows:

Roskrowe, in the hall

Two table boards with two old carpetts	4. 0. 0.
One court cupboard with his carpett	1. 0. 0.
One other cupboard	6. 8.
One small round table and one other with their carpetts	10. 0.
Two great tymber chayres	6. 8.
One dozen of joyne stooles	18. 0.
One dozen of old cushions	12. 0.
One greene broadcloth carpet, one other branches stuffe carpet[1] for the 2 long tables	16. 0.

Two payre of playing tables	5. 0.
One forme	1. 6.
One payre of andirons, shovell and tonges	13. 4.
Three paire of corselett, 2 holberts and one picke	1. 0. 0.

In the Parlor

One table board with a darnickes carpett[2]	1. 0. 0.

---

[1] 'branches stuffe': patterned fabric.
[2] 'darnickes': fabric originating at Doornick, a town in Flanders.

Fig. 46: Oak folding-top gate-leg table carved with lunettes and with applied ornament. Second quarter of the 17th Century; width about 91·5 cm. (Mallett & Son Ltd.)

One round table and one other small table	10. 0.
One old court cupboard	5. 0.
Seaven joyne stooles	7. 0.
Six cushions	4. 0.
Three other old cushions	1. 0.
One greate tymber chayre and 3 small ones	8. 0.
One paire of andirons with shovell and tongs	6. 8.
One paire of snuffers	6.

Elsewhere in the house, 'In the Chamber

over the Parler', was a chest of silver which included 'One basen and ewer parcell gilt' valued at £15, while in a closet were an unspecified number of 'small East Indea dishes' which were valued together with other vaguely described pieces of glass and pottery at £1. In the principal bedroom of the house there was little in the way of furniture:

One beadsteede furnished	18. 0. 0.
One truckell bead furnished	4. 0. 0.
2 stooles, 3 chayres all covered sutinge to the bead	1. 10. 0.
One court cupboard	2. 0. 0.

In addition there was a chest of clothing, the chest of plate mentioned above, five

Fig. 47: Oak cupboard in two stages, the upper part carved with floral and vine patterns and with rosettes. Mid-17th Century; width 185·5 cm. (Mary Bellis.)

cushions and a quilt and some fireirons. The wearing apparel was in a chest made of cypress wood, used for its resistance to attack by both woodworm, and more important under the circumstances, to moth.

Alexander Pendarves, a descendant of Samuel Pendarves, married Mary Granville in 1718. She was eighteen at the time, her partner was many years her senior and the young woman, later to re-marry following the death of her husband, became famous under the name of Mrs Delany. She wrote of her arrival at Roskrow with great sadness noting:

> I was led into an old hall that had scarce any light belonging to it; on the left hand of which was a parlour, the floor of which was rotten in places, and part of the ceiling broken down. . . .

She added that the house had not been inhabited for thirty years, so it is not unlikely that she was seeing it more or less as it was in 1643.

The furniture at Roskrow in the 17th

Above, Fig. 48: Oak table, the frieze carved with a stylised flower, leaf and snake pattern and the supports turned. Mid-17th Century; height 81·3 cm. (Christie's, London.)

Right, Fig. 49: Oak joint stool, the frieze moulded and punched. Mid-17th Century; width 47·5 cm. (Private collection.)

century is only briefly described, but it would appear to have been largely of Tudor type, with its court cupboards and joint stools. Such pieces were, nonetheless, still being made in the 1640's, although they differed in details of design from earlier examples. As in the first quarter of the century, supports were in the form of simple turnings with no ornament other than perhaps an encircling shallow ring. Carved motifs were mostly conventionalised flowers and leaves, with a common use of trailing vines and grapes. These are occasionally to be found decorating chairbacks, cupboards and, somewhat inappropriately, bed posts.

The furniture of the Roskrow bedroom is interesting; not only did the hangings match the covering of the chairs, but there was also a truckle bed. A contemporary diarist, who inquisitively went into a room where the maids were bed-making, 'espied little trundel beds under the greate beds, which he understood were for the gentlemen's men'. The truckles would have been fitted with wheels so that they could be pushed out of the way when not in use. Some of them were little more than a simple wooden support for a mattress, but others perhaps had a detachable framework to carry hangings. From the value of the example quoted, it was most probably of the latter type. Such beds continued to be mentioned from time to time for a further century or so, by which date it was more usual for masters and servants to have separate quarters.

IT has been mentioned earlier that most furniture-making was the province of joiners, sometimes assisted in their task by their fellow-woodworkers, the turners.

Below, *Fig. 50: Oak table, the frieze carved with an arcade pattern and the supports turned in the form of inverted balusters. Mid-17th Century; height 81·3 cm. (L. G. G. Ramsey Esq., F.S.A.)*

Right, *Fig. 51: Oak cupboard, the panelled door carved with a scroll pattern bordered by lunettes. Mid-17th Century; width about 124 cm.*

Occasionally, the latter made some on their own, and an example is illustrated in Fig. 40. Made from ash and dating from sometime in the 17th Century, it is carefully fitted together but without the use of mortice and tenon. Chairs of the type vary from one another in design, the more complex being laden with rings of wood hanging from various parts. Probably country-made to a traditional pattern, they are difficult to date with exactitude and it has been thought that most of them originated on the Welsh border. In 1761 they were being sought for Strawberry Hill, and Horace Walpole wrote to a friend asking him to find some for him. In his letter he described exactly what he wanted and the price he might have to pay:

> Dicky Bateman has picked up a whole cloister full of old chairs in Herefordshire—he bought them one by one, here and there in farm-houses, for three-and-sixpence and a crown apiece.

They are of wood, the seats triangular, the backs, arms, and legs loaded with turnery. A thousand to one but there are plenty up and down Cheshire too—.

These turned armchairs are sometimes called 'thrown' chairs, because they were made on a lathe for which the ancient name was a 'throwe'. Nowadays they are much scarcer than they were in 1761, and it will be found that they cost more.

Almost as uninviting as the foregoing to a tired man is the chair table. It is an early example of combining two pieces of furniture in one, and is known under various names: 'table-chair', 'table-chairwise' and 'monk's chair-table'. The last connexion with monasteries is no more than a figment of some unknown imagination; no

Below, *Fig. 52: Hanging food cupboard with turned bars and chip-carved framing. Mid-17th Century; width about 84 cm. (Mary Bellis.)* **Right,** *Plate 8: Carved and inlaid oak cupboard dating from the first half of the 17th Century; width 147·3 cm. (Temple Newsam House, Yorkshire: Leeds City Art Gallery.)*

doubt an attempt to impress on a buyer that he owned, or had an opportunity of owning, the one-time seat of some benign brother. Larger, similarly designed pieces are often called 'monk's benches' by the same reasoning.

The chair table is generally a clumsy object, heavily built from oak, and like some other convertible pieces is rarely satisfactory in either of its rôles. It would appear that they were popular in the 17th Century, and some dated examples survive from the first half. The chair shown in Fig. 41 is seen as a table in Fig. 42, and dates from about 1650. It is devoid of carving or inlay, and relies for decoration on shaped, pierced and moulded ornament applied to the back and elsewhere.

While stools and chairs were plentiful during the reign of Charles I, a larger article, the settle, was also popular. Again, usually made of oak, it has a tall upright back, an enclosed base with one or two hinged lids forming the seat, and arms of curved shape resting on turned or square supports. It is, in fact a long chest fitted with arms and a back, and forms a useful, if sometimes ungainly, piece of furniture. Its ancestry goes back to medieval times, but pre-1600 specimens are very scarce because many of them were fixed to walls and were destroyed when buildings were altered or demolished. A description of one of particularly intriguing design is in the inventory of the contents of Tart Hall, taken in 1641, which reads:

> a great settle bedstead in fashion of a fourme.

Quite different from any other English chair of the period is the specimen illustrated in Fig. 44, carved in pinewood, finished with light-coloured paint and partly gilt. It was formerly in Holland House, the Jacobean mansion set in a small park off High Street, Kensington, London. The house was destroyed by bombing in the 1940's, but its appearance and contents are recorded. Of the interior, it was noted by Walpole in

his *Anecdotes of Painting in England*, published between 1762 and 1771, that some of the work had been executed by Francis Cleyn. He was born at Rostock, a city on the Baltic, in 1582, and after spending some years in the service of Christian IV of Denmark came to England. Cleyn was recommended to Charles when Prince of Wales by Sir Henry Wotton, and James I appointed him official artist at the tapestry manufactory newly-opened at Mortlake. He is known to have painted four pictures inset in the walls of the North Drawing Room at Ham House, Surrey, which are listed in an inventory of 1683 as being by 'Decline'.

On his work at Holland House, Walpole, who was using material gathered by the early 18th-Century antiquary George Vertue, prints a tantalizingly brief paragraph:

> There is still extant a beautiful chamber adorned by him at Holland-house, with a ceiling in grotesque, and small compartments on the chimneys, in the style, and not unworthy, of Parmegiano. Two chairs, carved and gilt, with large shells for backs, belonging to the same room, were undoubtedly from his designs; and are evidences of his taste.

The grotesques 'not unworthy of Parmegiano' had vanished by 1874,[1] when an illustrated two-volume history of the house was published, and the walls of the room bore painted decoration from the hand of G. F. Watts; a friend of Lord and Lady Holland and an artist whose life spanned the years 1817 to 1904. The original ceiling collapsed at some time at the end of the 18th Century, so that none of the old work remained in the room.

An armchair of similar pattern to those once at Holland House, and presumed to have come from there, is in the Victoria and Albert Museum.

---

[1] *Princess Marie Liechtenstein*, Holland House, 2 vols., 1874.

5 : The Commonwealth

The abrupt termination of Charles I's reign in 1649 was followed by a period of upheaval throughout the British Isles. The Civil War led to loss of life and the destruction of property; great quantities of silver and gold articles were melted to

provide money for paying the two armies, and the religious fervour of the Puritans revenged itself on anything within range that was other than starkly functional or promised earthly pleasure.

In such circumstances, the furnishing of

Fig. 53: Illustrations to Randle Holme's Academy of Armory *prepared mainly between 1648 and 1649, and published in 1905. For key see text, page 72.*

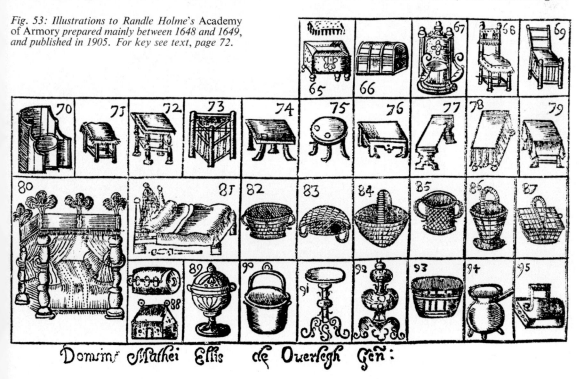

homes received little consideration. What had been current in the 1640's continued to be made, and for the best part of twenty years there was little or no change to be observed. Anyone requiring articles of new pattern would have to get them in some manner from across the sea, and in spite of difficulties this was achieved. Such extravagances were limited to the more affluent and enterprising, who made use of friends and relatives with overseas connexions and then waited anxiously in case misadventure on the water robbed them of their purchases.

Thus, in June 1652, John Evelyn, who had gone down to Rye, in Sussex, to meet his wife on her return from Paris, recorded:

> 11th. About 4 in yᵉ afternoone being at bowles on yᵉ grene, we discover'd a vessell, which prov'd to be that in which my Wife was, and which got into yᵉ harbour about 8 yᵗ evening to my no small joy. They had ben three days at sea, and escaped the Dutch fleete, thro' which they pass'd, taken for fishers, wᶜʰ was great good fortune, there being 17 bailes of furniture and other rich plunder, wᶜʰ I blesse God came all safe to land, together wᵗʰ my Wife, and my Lady Browne her Mother, who accompanied her.

The family home of the Verney family, Claydon House, Buckinghamshire, suffered damage during the Civil War; its owner, Ralph Verney, having gone abroad in 1643 rather than sign the Covenant agreeing to religious practice 'according to the word of God and the example of the best reformed churches'. He returned to England in 1653, bringing with him Venetian looking-glasses and Dutch cabinets, together with fabrics and fringes for hangings and for upholstering furniture.

There are other references in documents to purchases of the same kind being made outside the country. Even when the opposing forces had been disbanded, conditions were far from conducive to commissioning or making decorative objects, and

until a sovereignty had been re-established and accepted there was little alternative to importing all such requirements with the exception of commonplace ones. The sole innovation in the way of decorative ornament took the form of inlay in mother-of-pearl and bone or ivory, but the work was executed on articles of current heavy

Opposite, *Plate 9: Walnut settee with turned ornament and red velvet upholstery. Circa 1660; width 170 cm. (Montacute House, Somerset: The National Trust.)*

Below, *Fig. 54: Oak chair, the shaped cross-members in the back carved with scrolls centred on male heads. Yorkshire, circa 1660. (N. Horton-Fawkes, Esq., Farnley Hall, Yorkshire.)*

pattern and much of the gaiety of appearance otherwise attainable was therefore lacking (Figs. 62, 63).

An idea of the contents of a home of the period is to be gained from a book written at the time: Randle Holme's *Academy of Armory*. Holme studied heraldry, held the post of deputy-Garter for Cheshire, Shropshire, Lancashire and North Wales, and lived from 1627 to 1699. The first part of his book was issued in 1688, but the second did not appear until 1905, when it was edited by I. H. Jeayes and printed in a small edition by the Roxburghe Club. The original manuscript is among the Harleian collection in the British Museum, and totals ten volumes, from which a few sections of the original work are missing.

Holme's book is sub-titled *A Storehouse of Armory and Blazon*, and in it the author contrives to link everyday objects with heraldry. In places his ingenuity fails him, and in a section devoted to the sea, with descriptions of parts of the ship and marine terms in general, he makes little or no attempt to relate them to blazonry. The whole is stated to have been prepared in 1648–9, and although it is not improbable that some of the definitions were amended prior to the printing of forty years later, the words and pictures are relevant to the English home at both the beginning and end of the third quarter of the 17th Century.

Interspersed among other matter are the following lists, which detail the contents of the principal rooms in a house:

Things necessary for and belonging to a dineing Rome.
The Rome well wanscoted about, either with Moontan [muntin: the vertical member between panels] and panells or carved as the old fashion was; or else in larg square panell.
The Rome hung with pictures of all sorts, as History, Landskips, Fancyes, &c.
Larg Table in the midle, either square to draw out in Leaves, or Long, or Round or oval with falling leaves.

Side tables, or court cubberts, for cups and Glasses to drink in, Spoons, Sugar Box, Viall and Cruces for Viniger, Oyle and Mustard pot.
Cistern of Brass, Pewter, or Lead to set flagons of Beer, and Bottles of win in.

Opposite, Fig. 55: Oak armchair, the back inset with a panel carved in a formal vine pattern and surmounted by pierced scrolls. Yorkshire/Derbyshire type, c. 1640; height 106·6 cm. (Temple Newsam House, Yorkshire: Leeds City Art Gallery.)

Below, Fig. 56: Oak armchair, the back shaped at top and sides and inset with a carved panel above which is the date 1661. (Mary Bellis.)

Fig. 57: *Oak armchair, the cresting and apron ornamented with turned balls.* *Mid-17th Century.* (*L. G. G. Ramsey, Esq., F.S.A.*)

A Turky table couer, or carpett of cloth or Leather printed. Chaires and stooles of Turky work, Russia or calves Leather, cloth or stuffe, or of needlework. Or els made all of Joynt work or cane chaires.

Fire grate, fire shovell, Tongs, and Land Irons all adorned with Brass Bobbs and Buttons.

Flower potts, or Allabaster figures to adorn the windows, and glass well painted and a Larg seeing Glass at the higher end of the Rome.

A Faire with-drawing Rome at the other end of the dineing Rome well furnished with a Table, Chaires and stooles &c.

Things usefull about a Bed, and bed-chamber.

Bed stocks, as Bed posts, sides, ends, Head and Tester.

Mat, or sack-cloth bottom.

Cord, Bed staves, and stay or the feet.

Curtain Rods and hookes, and rings, either Brass or Horn.

Beds, of chaffe, Wool or flocks, Feathers, and down in Ticks or Bed Tick.

Bolsters, pillows.

Blankets, Ruggs, Quilts, Counterpan, cad-dows [rough woolen covers].

Curtaines, Valens, Tester Head cloth; all either fringed, Laced or plaine alike.

Inner curtaines and Valens, which are generally White silk or Linen.

Tester Bobbs of Wood gilt, or couered sutable to the curtaines.

Tester top either flatt, or Raised, or canopy like, or half Testered.

Basis, or the lower Valens at the seat of the Bed, which reacheth to the ground, and fringed for state as the vper Valens, either with Inch fring, caul fring, Tufted fring, snailing fring, Gimpe fring with Tufts and Buttons, Vellem fring, &c.

The Chamber.

Hangings about the Rome, of all sorts, as Arras, Tapestry, damask, silk, cloth or stuffe: in paines or with Rods, or gilt Leather, or plaine, else Pictures of Friends and Relations to Adorne the Rome.

Table, stands, dressing Box with drawers, a larg Myrour, or Looking glass. Couch, chaire, stoles, and chaires, a closs-stole.

Window curtaines, Flower Potts.

Fire grate, and a good Fire in the winter, Fire shovel, Tongs, Fork and Bellowes.

Right, Fig. 59: Oak chest-cupboard with hinged lid and a pair of doors below, the inset panels at the front carved with lozenge-shaped patterns and the frieze fluted. Mid-17th Century. (Mary Bellis.)

Holme gave the undermentioned descriptions of the items he illustrated, but his heraldic comments have been omitted in view of their lack of relevance in the present instance:[1]

65. A jewel-box with gilt metal lock and feet; 'This kind of cabinett is such as Ladyes keepe their rings, necklaces, Braclett, and Jewells In: it stands constantly on the table (called the dressing table) in their Bed chamber.'

66. A chest; 'These kind of coffers and trunks were first invented to be thus garded by old vsurers, or couetous Misers, to keep safely that treasure committed to it, as vnto a castle strongly fortified. . . . If it haue a streight, and flat couer, it is called a Chest. . . .'.

67. A throne; 'a chair Royall . . . adorned with veriaty of precious stones . . .'.

68. A chair; 'made vp by an Imbrautherer' in Turkey-work or needlework, and alternatively known as a stool-chair or a back-stool.

69. A turned chair.

70. 'Some term it a settle chaire, being so weighty that it cannot be moued from place to place . . . haueing a kind of box or cubbert in the seate of it'.

71. A stool.

72. A joint stool; according to Holme known in most of Cheshire as a buffet stool.

73. A turned stool; 'wrought with Knops, and rings all ouer the feete, these and the chaires are generally made with three feete . . .'.

74. A country stool; 'or Block stoole, being onely a thick peece of wood, with either 3 or 4 peece of wood fastned in it for feet.'

75. 'A countrey stoole made round with three feete . . .'.

---

[1]*Holme was rarely lost for a suitable example. He noted of a three-footed stool (75): 'Argent such a stoole sable is borne by* Die Schoner Van Sturben-hart, *a Germane family'; of a joint-form he stated 'Gules the like Joynt forme in fesse between 3 flowers de lis Argent is borne by* De la Barnach *in France.'*

Below, *Fig. 60: Oak cupboard with recessed upper part flanked by turned corner supports, the doors with applied lozenge-shaped mouldings on the sunken panels. First half of the 17th Century; width 142·2 cm. (L. G. G. Ramsey, Esq., F.S.A.)*

76. 'A nursing stoole . . . in some places it
   is called a crickett, or low stoole, or a
   child's stoole . . .'.
77. A joint-form; 'some are made with
   turned feete, 4 or 6, according to its
   length, haueing railes or Barres both
   aboue, for the seate to be fixed vpon,
   and below, to hold the feete firme and
   stiddy'.
78. A long table covered with a cloth.
79. A table couered with a carpet: 'some
   are covered with a carpett of Turky
   work, or needle worke or such like'.
80. 'A Bed Royall'. Holme admitted that
   he had never seen it in heraldry but
   knew of it as a shop sign in the city of
   London.
81. A bed with its blanket, bolster and sheet
   turned down; a type without a tester
   and known as a truckle bed 'because
   they trundle under other beds'. Beside
   it is a bed-staff, sometimes known as a
   burthen staff. Of the purpose of the
   latter there has been much argument,
   but probably they were stuck in holes
   at each side of the bed frame to prevent
   the mattress from falling off. The fact
   that Holme shows one as being apparently about 4ft. in length does not
   mean that they were anything like that
   size; he was unconcerned about proportions, as his no. 65 where a hair-brush
   is shown to be as big as a jewel-case.
82–7. Various types of basket, of which 86
   and 87 were used for carrying eggs and
   butter to market.
88. 'A Port Mantle' (portmanteau) and,
   below, an ark; 'a kind of little house
   made of wood and couered with haire
   cloth, and so by two rings hung in the
   midle of a Rome, thereby to secure all
   things put therein from the cruelty of
   devouring Rats, mice, Weesels, and
   such kind of Vermine'.
89–90. A covered cup and a 'kettle'.
91. A stand: 'a little round table, set vpon
   one pillar, or post, which in the foote
   branches it selfe out into three or
   foure feete or toes . . . it is used for to
   set a Bason on whilest washing, or a
   candle to read by . . .'.
92–5. Respectively, an 'And-Iron, or Land
   Iron', a tub, 'a Possnett', and a
   smoothing iron for the use of a Laun-
   dress.

*Opposite, Fig. 62: Chest of oak inlaid with engraved
bone and mother-of-pearl, and further decorated with
applied mouldings and split turnings. Dated 1662;
width 114·3 cm. (Montacute House, Somerset: The
National Trust.)* **Above,** *Fig. 63: Oak chest inlaid
with engraved bone and mother-of-pearl, decorated
with applied mouldings and split turnings. Circa
1660. (Mallett & Son Ltd.)*

The articles detailed and depicted by
Randle Holme would have been those
familiar to him and his contemporaries, and
would not have included any outside the
range of what was likely to exist in the
average dwelling. Probably there were
some variations in ornamental features, but
on the whole there was no dramatic change
during the half-century following 1600.

Doubtless the Puritan horror of display
was reflected in a diminution of carving and
inlay, and their replacement by sober-
looking applied mouldings to break-up flat
surfaces. It is most probable, however,
that in the uncertainties of the times, the
majority of people made the best of what
they possessed. Cromwell and his allies

were certainly not leaders of fashion, whatever else they may have been, so no innovations in style emanated from that quarter.

Dated furniture made in the period appears to be less in quantity than that surviving from the reigns of James I and Charles I, but their occupancies of the throne covered just under fifty years and the interregnum lasted for a bare dozen. Thus, it is not surprising that few pieces are extant with a positive record of their having been made between 1649 and 1660. From those few it has been possible to conjecture what was popular, but Holme remains the most useful source of information.

THE principal changes are to be noted in connexion with tables and chests. With the former, there was a liking for those with hinged tops supported by swinging 'gate' legs, and the supports either turned or flat and of waved outline to give a profile of turning. No doubt the principal table continued to be a heavily-built one of

planked-top refectory type or with withdrawing leaves, differing from those made earlier only in having less bulky legs.

Over the years the disadvantage of storing clothing in a chest had become apparent; accessible only by lifting the top, the contents were not only liable to become creased but those low down in the pile could only be reached with difficulty. When personal possessions had generally been few in number this inconvenience might have been acceptable, but as individual wealth increased simpler storage was demanded.

The drawer began to appear in the early decades of the 17th Century, and as the years passed its use grew more widespread. In some instances a chest with rising top was given one or two drawers in the base, a variation seen in the small-sized example

shown in Fig. 58 which is made more useful and attractive by being raised from the ground on turned supports. Somewhat more frequently seen are chests of earlier type measuring five feet or so in width, with two drawers side-by-side at floor level.

While the two-stage cupboard continued to be made in the mid-century, changes in its appearance are noticeable. The columns at either side of the upper part are either simple turnings or merely short knobs pendent from the top frieze. As exemplified in the cupboard illustrated in Fig. 60, doors were sometimes given shaped panelling of involved design. Uprights were emphasized by applying them with turnings, split lengthwise and giving scope to the man at the lathe in devising fresh combinations of bobbins, balusters and narrow rings. The present piece also boasts a full-width drawer faced with a length of gadroon carving, above the cupboard in the lower section.

In most cases drawers of this date have grooves cut along both of their sides, which are made to fit corresponding projecting strips within the carcase. The drawer must therefore be given linings thick enough to take the grooves, and is in this way suspended from them. A chest showing this type of construction is seen in Fig. 66 on page 83.

By the late 1650's a new type of decoration had been introduced and remained in favour for a decade or so. The plain panels inset within mouldings were inlaid with engraved bone and mother-of-pearl to form scrolling designs, and occasionally the applied turnings and mouldings were painted black to contrast with the plain wood background. The upper outside panels of the cabinet in Fig. 63 centre on arched bevelled frames, and it may be wondered whether they once enclosed small paintings to aid the deception of distance. Another cabinet, slightly later in date than the preceding example, is shown in Fig. 62. The outer drawers at the top bear the numerals *16* and *62* respectively, engraved

at the lower end of the central triangular motif, and presumably record the date of the article's manufacture.

The group of pieces in Fig. 64 comprises a dining table, a bench and two joint stools, all of them dating from the middle years of the 17th Century. The foremost of the stools has a frieze carved with lunettes, but the remaining items are of everyday plain types that must have existed once in large quantities. As they are seen, in a photograph taken in about 1920, they are completely unrestored and show every sign of having endured some 250 years of average use and mis-use. It is interesting to see them in this condition, clearly revealing likely areas for modern repair.

Single chairs of the time followed the design of the 'Farthingale' type, which originated in about 1615, with seats and backs covered in leather or needlework. Armchairs also copied earlier patterns, and examples are seen in Figs. 55–57 and 61. Fig. 56 is dated 1661, the back panel carved with a well-designed pattern of scrolling flowers; tulips and others all apparently springing from the same root. Another armchair (Fig. 61) features a row of turned uprights inset in the upper half of the back, the lower containing a carved panel. A third, Fig. 57, is unusual in having the cresting of the back and seat-rail embellished with turned balls.

6 : Charles II

ON 29th May 1660, his birthday, Charles II, who had been proclaimed King some days earlier, entered the city of London. John Evelyn wrote of the event and noted the tremendous enthusiasm with which his arrival was greeted:

> . . . with a triumph of above 20,000 horse and foote, brandishing their swords and shouting with inexpressible joy; the wayes strew'd with flowers, the bells ringing, the streetes hung with tapissry, fountaines running with wine; the Maior, Aldermen, and all the Companies in their liveries, chaines of gold, and banners; Lords and Nobles clad in cloth of silver, gold, and velvet; the windowes and balconies all set with ladies; trumpets, music and myriads of people flocking, even so far as from Rochester, so as they were seven houres in passing the citty, even from 2 in yᵉ afternoon till 9 at night.

His contemporary and fellow-diarist, Samuel Pepys, was much concerned in the arrangements for bringing Charles to England, and had travelled on one of the ships that went to The Hague to fetch him. After landing at Dover, the King continued his journey and on the day of his entry into London, when Evelyn was in the Strand,

Pepys was out on horseback at Deal, betting with his companions about the height of a cliff. Finding the local people lighting a bonfire and firing guns to celebrate the Royal birthday, he 'did give twenty shillings among them to drink'.

Fig. 65: Oak-lined drawer showing dove-tailed corner, and runner.

What John Evelyn, and doubtless many others, too, described as 'calamitous sufferings' had come to an end. Charles had left his native land in 1646; then having returned to live briefly and uneasily in Scotland, was defeated at Worcester and went to France. Short of money, he lived for a time in Paris, then in Cologne, Middleburg, Bruges, Brussels and Breda, while friends and enemies plotted for and

against his return. If nothing else, his unhappy sojourn enabled him to see how others lived, and this fact, together with his mother's French blood and the annual revenue of £1,300,000 granted to him by a grateful and hopeful Parliament, portended considerable changes at Whitehall.

The changes were followed eagerly by most of those who saw or knew of them, and must have appeared a symbol of optimism which would help to deaden recollection of recent tragic years. Inevitably, the sudden release from the dreary asceticism of the preceding decade led to a big swing of the pendulum in the opposite direction. It was reflected on the stage in the lively comedies of Wycherley, Congreve and others, and in fashionable homes by a transformation in appearance and comfort.

While innovations in furnishing were accepted quickly by the well-to-do, it would have taken many years before they percolated through to ordinary homes had the Great Fire of London not taken place. The conflagration broke out at that memorably-named spot Pudding Lane, and Samuel Pepys carefully recorded much of what occurred in a series of graphic diary entries. He noted on the morning of Sunday, 2nd September 1666, a matter of twelve hours or so after the start of the blaze, after going by boat to the east of London Bridge:

> Everybody endeavouring to remove their goods, and flinging into the river, or bringing them into lighters that lay off; poor people staying in their houses as long as till the very fire touched them, and then running into boats, or clambering from one pair of stairs, by the waterside, to another.

Later on the same day he walked along Watling Street:

> as well as I could, every creature coming away loaden with goods to save, and here and there sick people carried away in beds.

After having his dinner he was again out and about, noticing in the city:

the streets full of nothing but people and horses and carts loaden with goods, ready to run over one another, and removing goods from one burned house to another.
. . . River full of lighters and boats taking in goods, and good goods swimming in the water; and only I

Opposite, *Fig. 67: Walnut armchair with barley-twist turned supports, the back cresting carved with cupids supporting a crown and the front rail with a crown; stamped beneath the seat-rail* RP, *probably the mark of Richard Price who is known to have supplied chairs and stools to Charles II. Circa 1680; height 116·8 cm. (Temple Newsam House: Leeds City Art Gallery.)*

Below, *Fig. 68: Walnut chair with caned seat and back, carved on the cresting and front rail with cupids supporting crowns; stamped* RB, *perhaps for Richard Bealing. Circa 1690; height 119·4 cm. (Temple Newsam House: Leeds City Art Gallery.)*

observed that hardly one lighter or boat in three that had the goods of a house in, but there was a pair of virginals in it.

Pepys himself emptied his house and sent the contents away to safety to a friend's home in the country, and the removal of furnishings from Whitehall Palace was begun. Finally, the authorities gained command of the situation, and by blowing up buildings in the path of the fire it was eventually extinguished. It laid waste 13,200 houses and 460 streets covering an area of 436 acres, the value of the destruction being given at the time as between seven and ten million pounds.[1]

Temporary housing in the form of huts was erected on many of the open spaces then surrounding the city, and John Evelyn wrote of how

> the poore inhabitants were dispers'd about St. George's Fields, and Moorefields, as far as Highgate, and severall miles in circle, some under tents, some under miserable hutts and hovells, many without a rag or any necessary utensills, bed or board, who from delicatenesse, riches, and easy accomodations in stately and well furnish'd houses, were now reduc'd to extreamest misery and poverty.

There can be no doubt that a large proportion of the former city-dwellers lost all or most of their possessions. Once the re-building got under way and re-housing began, there must have been a considerable call for new furniture. It would have been demanded in the styles then fashionable, embodying recently-introduced improvements in construction.

Hitherto, furniture-making had remained the prerogative of the joiner and the turner, with the former in the ascendant. The mortice and tenon joint had served well for straightforward box-like chests, for the frames of tables, chairs and stools, but for more elegant and light-weight articles, better was needed. This was especially so for pieces fitted with drawers and suffering continual wear and tear, and which demanded therefore new techniques of manufacture. As a result, the dovetail joint, which comprises a series of tenons in the shape of the bird's tail, was improved and came into general use. It had been employed in a coarse form for a century or so,

Below, *Fig. 69; Walnut chair with turned supports and leather seat and back. Probably Flemish;* circa *1670; height 88·3 cm. (Montacute House, Somerset: The National Trust.)*

Opposite, *Fig. 70: Cabinet veneered with walnut and inlaid with panels of floral marquetry, the stand fitted with drawers and raised on barley-twist legs united by openworked stretchers.* Circa *1680; width about 120 cm. (Mallett & Son Ltd.)*

---

[1] See J. C. Timbs, Curiosities of London, *1868, pages 338–41.*

but now was made neater and stronger by giving it more dovetails along a given length and cutting them with greater precision.

At the same time, the earlier method of grooving the sides of a drawer to fit a corresponding bearer in the carcase was abandoned in favour of runners. They were fixed at each side of the bottom of the space where a drawer fitted, so that it would slide or run along them with ease. A reinforcing strip was placed in the angle between the drawer-side and drawer-bottom, so that there was a narrow flat running surface to make a good fit with friction-free travel (Fig. 65). In time the angle-pieces and runners wear down, the drawer becomes loose in the space provided for it and will tend to tip when opened, but the condition can be corrected by replacing the strips of wood beneath the drawer-bottom and renewing the runners.

Whereas an increasing number of chests and cabinets had hitherto been fitted with drawers, from 1660 onwards those without them became a minority. The chest of drawers soon became standardized with two short (or narrow) drawers at the top and three long, wide ones below.

Twisted or 'barley-sugar' turning was introduced from the other side of the English Channel, and was popular not only for the legs of cabinets, but for those of tables, chairs and stools as well as for the uprights of chair-backs. The most common are of simple form, closely resembling the sticks of barley-sugar from which their name has been derived. Others are double twists with a space running between the two opposed turns, but although attractive in appearance they were far from strong and genuine examples are now scarce.

Turned work of these types was seldom carried out in oak, which the tools of the time were inadequate to manage satisfactorily, but was most successful in walnut. While the tree grew in England and native timber was usable, most of the requirements for furniture-making were imported from France. There are references to 'Grenoble' walnut, and the wood was highly recommended by John Evelyn in his book *Sylva, or a Discourse of Forest Trees*, published in 1664. He said of it:

. . . were this Timber in greater plenty amongst us, we should have far better Utensils of all sorts for our Houses, as Chairs, Stools, Bedsteads, Tables, Wainscot [wall-panelling], Cabinets, &c. in stead of more vulgar Beech, subject to the worm, weak, and unsightly. . . .

Beech-wood, although it was vulnerable to attack by wood-worm, was a much less costly timber than walnut and many others, and was used at all periods. The grain has been described aptly as 'featureless', and as it has an absorbent surface it was often painted and stained to resemble something more costly and attractive.

Walnut is appreciated for its warm brown colour and distinctive black markings, and to make the most of the wood it was, and still is, usually cut in veneers: very thin slices which are glued into place. In this form, the craftsman is able to select the pieces with the most attractive features and arrange them, if desired, in patterns. These often take the form of four identically marked veneers arranged on a surface so that the markings radiate or form a diamond. Known as 'quartering', it employs four pieces cut successively from a log and

Fig. 73: Table veneered with 'oysters' of walnut and raised on barley-twist turned supports united by an 'X'-shaped stretcher. Circa 1680. (Mallett & Son Ltd.)

thus all bearing the same pattern; each is on a very slightly smaller scale than the one below it, but this is scarcely noticeable.

Hitherto the joiner had taken his wood and fashioned it as required, and any ornament took the form of carving, painting and a small amount of rough inlay in contrastingly-coloured material. Almost simultaneously with the accession of Charles II a big development occurred: the wood itself began to be employed in a decorative manner. Formerly, it had been cut and no attempt was made to take advantage of its natural features in the way of distinctive markings or particularly attractive areas of colour, but now a method had been found of doing so.

Veneering meant that costly timber was employed to the utmost and waste reduced to a minimum. It was found that pine-wood was easy to work, cheap, reasonably durable and, above all, made an excellent surface to which veneer might be glued and remain affixed. Very rarely used for furniture unless it was disguised in some way, such as by painting, pine was imported from the Baltic area, and is nowadays often known as Deal. The latter term was explained by Thomas Sheraton in 1803, who noted:

> DEAL, from *Deel*, Dutch for a part, quantity, or degree of, more or less. Hence, fir or pine timber being cut into thin portions, they are called deals.

Thus, the word originally referred to a size of plank and later was corrupted into a name for the wood.

WITH the introduction of more sophisticated techniques a new and more skilful craftsman came into being. Not only did his ideas, such as details of construction and ornamentation, come from other countries, but most of the newly-introduced types of furniture originated similarly. French and Dutch workers came to London to practise their skill, and although resented by those long-established in the city they stimulated the latter to improve their workmanship. Predictably the immigrants made articles very similar to those they had been making in their native lands, and it is not always possible to be definite about the precise origin of some of their work. The problem-pieces might have been made, say, in Holland, in England by the same man on his arrival there, or even in the latter country by a skilful Englishman closely following a Dutch prototype. In some instances, such pieces will never be attributed to everyone's satisfaction and today, more often than not, they are usually accepted, with resignation, as having been made in whichever of the contending countries the particular article happens to be.

The technique of marquetry is in reality an extension of veneering. In it, veneers of contrastingly marked and coloured woods, and sometimes different materials such as bone and mother-of-pearl, were assembled to form a pattern and then glued down. In many instances light-coloured woods, like holly, were stained green to simulate leaves, the veins being indicated by incisions. John Evelyn mentions in *Sylva* that

> When they would imitate the naturall turning of leaves in their curious compartiments and bordures of flower works, they effect it by dipping the pieces so far into hot sand as they would have the shadow.

The art was brought to England from Holland, where it reached a very high standard. The Dutch frequently used their love of flowers as an inspiration for designs, and the doors of cabinets and tops of tables bore elaborate representations of vases crammed with all kinds of blooms. Closely similar work was executed in both countries, but only rarely did the English 'markatree' equal that of the Dutch, whose great skill at the art gave their 'pictures' a noticeably more realistic appearance.

Chairs of the time showed changes that make them immediately distinguishable from earlier types. They have disproportionately tall backs, and backward-sloping rear legs; the latter feature giving increased stability to balance the somewhat ungainly height, but being retained in future years when the back became lower. Many such chairs were of walnut, but a large number of the surviving specimens are of beech which was painted black. This may have been done to hide the nature of the wood or to protect it from worm, and it has proved surprisingly successful in both functions.

Below, *Fig. 74: Oak folding-top gate-leg table, the turned under-framing linked by a flat 'X'-shaped stretcher. Circa 1670; width about 153 cm. (Mary Bellis.)* **Right,** *Fig. 75: Oak folding gate-leg table with tapering fluted baluster legs, moulded stretchers and knurled feet. Circa 1680; width 78·7 cm. (Temple Newsam House: Leeds City Art Gallery.)*

They could be finished in two fashions: with cane or fabric. Caning was employed to fill a panel in the back as well as for the seat, and to the latter a loose cushion was doubtless added. The expanses of back and seat were much larger when intended for covering and offered considerable scope to the upholsterer, who was coming into his own in ministering to the demands for comfort. Fabrics of many varieties were home-manufactured as well as imported: from Italy came silk velvets, figured and plain, and damask, but French workers were apparently active in England as early as 1663. A pamphlet issued in that year drew attention to 'the vast multitudes of Broad and narrow silk weavers, makers of . . . fringes . . .', but many ladies employed themselves with the needle and provided their own coverings for chairs and other furnishings. At Badminton, Gloucestershire, a visitor to the house shortly after the Restoration saw the females of the family busily working 'upon Embroidery and fringemaking; for all the beds of state were made and finished in the house'.

Stools which matched in pattern the lower parts of chairs were also made, and there is evidence that for formal occasions they continued to outnumber more comfortable seating arrangements. The account of the travels in England in 1669 of Cosimo III, Duke of Tuscany, written by his secretary, records his visit to the Earl of Pembroke, at Wilton, near Salisbury. In one of the rooms

> There was prepared for his highness, at the head of the table, an arm-chair which he insisted upon the young lady's taking; upon which the earl instantly drew forward another similar one, on which the serene prince sat, in the highest place, all the rest sitting on stools.

On the same tour, when at the Earl of Sunderland's mansion, Althorp, Northamptonshire, the Duke was again offered an armchair,

he having previously desired that my lady, the wife of the Earl, might be seated in a similar one; the Earl also was obliged by his highness to take his place close to him, the gentlemen of the retinue sitting separately on stools.[1]

Couches and day-beds, the latter in appearance usually a backless single-ended version of the couch, had been made in small numbers since the Middle Ages. The two were often confused by contemporaneous writers, but they agree on its purpose as a convenient full length resting-place employed thus during the day-time for short periods. Stuart examples followed the patterns of chairs, and in the case of the day-bed the end often sloped outwards and was hinged so that it might be adjusted to a comfortable angle.

A combination of both day-bed and couch is the so-called 'Knole Settee', a modernised version of a unique early 17th-Century piece at Knole. Upholstered in crimson velvet trimmed with silk fringe, it has arms at each end and above them are hinged cushioned headrests. Equally remarkable for their age and provident preservation are two armchairs of Charles II date at Ham House, on the outskirts of London. They have 'wings' at each side of the back, while the latter adjusts by means of a ratchet. In an inventory of the contents taken in 1679 they are listed as '2 sleeping chayres, carv'd and guilt frames, covered with crimson & gould stuff with gould fringe'.

Tables of all kinds were made, with the

---

[1] *Quoted by Francis Lenygon (Margaret Jourdain) in* Furniture in England from 1660 to 1760, *1914, page 5.*

old style of loose-topped refectory vieing for popularity with folding gate-legs. The latter survive in large and small sizes, and contemporary reports note that it was the fashionable custom to seat guests in groups at several small tables rather than at one big one. There is also Samuel Pepys's note of a pioneer expanding example, which he recorded in May 1665, as follows:

> To Sir Phillip Warwick's to dinner, where abundance of company came in unexpectedly; and here saw one pretty

piece of household stuff, as the company increaseth, to put a larger leaf upon an oval table.

Much ingenuity was exercised in the design of turned supports, with combinations of bobbins, balusters and spirals; alternatively, flat uprights were given a waved edge to simulate the outline of 'barley-sugar' twist, and some of the larger examples had a pair of gates at each side so as to provide the maximum steadiness. In addition to tables for dining, there was a mode for others that were purely decorative, comparatively small in size and usually fitted with a single drawer in the front (Fig. 73). Many were given marquetry ornament and raised on turned legs linked at the base by a shaped cross-stretcher.

Fig. 76: Oak table on turned supports, the flaps raised on hinged arms (lopers). Late 17th Century; width about 70 cm. (Mary Bellis.)

7 : James II, William and Mary

CHARLES died in 1685 and was succeeded by his brother, James, Duke of York, who reigned as James II. His few years on the throne were marked by religious controversy, which had never completely died down, and his open profession of catholicism led to his eventual expulsion from the country. The Dutch-born William of Orange, son of Charles I's daughter, was married to Mary, the daughter of James II, so both were related to the banished sovereign. William, a valorous man who had directed the battles of Holland against France was, above all, an avowed Protestant, and was invited to accept the English throne. He and his wife were crowned King and Queen in 1689, and following Mary's death in 1694, William reigned alone for a further eight years.

So much for the bare bones of history, but the pattern of furniture-design had been set at the Restoration and the ensuing upheavals, major and minor, did little noticeably to alter it. Earlier, in 1683, John Evelyn was at Whitehall Palace, and recorded his impressions of the luxury with which the King's French-born mistress, Louise de Keroualle, was surrounded. He wrote:

Following his Majesty this morning thro' the gallerie, I went, with the few who attended him, into the Duchesse of Portsmouth's *dressing-roome* within her bed-chamber, where she was in her morning loose garment, her maids combing her, newly out of her bed, his Ma^{ty} and the gallants standing about her; but that which engag'd my curiosity was the rich and splendid furniture of this woman's apartment, now twice or thrice pull'd down and rebuilt to satisfie her prodigal and expensive pleasures, whilst her Ma^{tys} does not exceede some gentlemen's ladies in furniture and accomodation. Here I saw the new fabriq of French tapissry, for designe, tendernesse of worke, and incomparable imitation of the best paintings, beyond any thing I had ever beheld. . . . Then for Japan cabinets, screenes, pendule clocks, greate vases of wrought plate, tables, stands, chimney furniture, sconces, branches, braseras [braziers], &c. all of massie silver, and out of number, besides some of her Ma^{tys} best paintings.

Evelyn points out that in his opinion the Duchess enjoyed comforts far greater than those of the Queen and her subjects. It was, however, an age when ostentation manifested itself in both clothing and furnishing, and the critics of extravagance,

Left, *Plate 13: Looking-glass in a carved and silvered wood frame, the cresting centred on the coat of arms of Gough of Old Fallings Hall and Perry Hall, Staffordshire. Circa 1670; height 176·5 cm. (Victoria and Albert Museum.)*

Right, *Fig. 77: Cabinet on stand, veneered with West Indian* lignum vitae *and ornamented with embossed silver mounts and escutcheons; one of a pair presented to Queen Henrietta Maria, consort of Charles I, by Henry Jermyn, Earl of St. Albans, who was successively her vice-Chamberlain, Master of Horse, secretary, and Commander of the Queen's Bodyguard. Circa 1665; width 151 cm. (Windsor Castle: reproduced by gracious permission of Her Majesty the Queen.)*

while vocal, went largely unheeded. It is doubtful if such excesses as the silver bedstead presented by the King to Nell Gwyn were considered worthy of imitation, or as being the most admirable way of disposing of the Royal income.

The bedstead, which disappeared long ago, is known to have been made by a foreign-named silversmith, John Cooqus, at a cost of £906. 7s. 5d. Probably much of it was formed of timber covered with thin plates of embossed and engraved metal, as were tables and some other articles made at the time and still surviving. Two such tables and other pieces are at Windsor Castle, and a suite of table, two candle-stands and a mirror, dating between 1676 and 1680, is at Knole, Kent. Another suite, of walnut mounted with silver plaques, now in the Metropolitan Museum, New York, was sold by auction in London in 1928 and realised what was then a sensational price of 10,100 guineas (£10,605: $25, 452,at $2.40 to the £).

A few similar pieces are mentioned in diaries and other records, but have since been sold for their silver value. Some were once at Bretby Hall, Derbyshire, a house that was demolished and subsequently rebuilt. It was visited in about 1700 by the indefatigable traveller and diarist, Celia Fiennes, who wrote:

> I was in severall bed Chambers, one had a crimson damaske bed, y[e] other Crimson velvet set upon halfe paces: this best was y[e] bride Chamber w[ch] used to be Call'd y[e] Silver roome where y[e] stands, table and fire utensills were all massy silver, but when plaite was in nomination to pay a tax, y[e] Earle of Chesterfield sold it all and y[e] plaite of y[e] house.[1]

'Fire utensills' comprising shovels, tongs and bellows, may be seen at Ham House, just outside London, where they have remained since they were made in about 1675.

Furnishings for the Royal palaces, as well

---

[1] Through England on a Side Saddle in the Time of William and Mary, *1888, page 141.*

as for such dignitaries as the Lord-Lieutenant of Ireland, the Lord-President of Wales and Ambassadors stationed abroad, were provided by the King's Great Wardrobe. It was under the control of a Master, or Keeper, and assistants, who in time acquired a Controller, a Surveyor, and a varying number of tradesmen and artificers who were 'all sworn servants to the King'. The duties and importance of the Wardrobe were increased by James I, and it was then housed in a mansion off Carter Lane, in the city, the building being flanked by the church of St. Andrew by the Wardrobe. Both were destroyed in the Great Fire of 1666, but while the church was rebuilt by Wren, the Wardrobe was removed westwards to the Savoy.

In the third quarter of the 17th Century the Master was Ralph Montagu, son of Lord Montagu of Boughton House, Northamptonshire, (later created first Duke of Montagu), who held the office from 1671 to 1685 and again from 1689 to 1695. On a prior occasion, during the years 1618–22, the Master was Lionel Cranfield, later Earl of Middlesex, whose daughter married the fifth Earl of Dorset. Their son, the sixth Earl, held the Office of Lord Chamberlain from 1689 to 1697, and at his seat, Knole, there remain today some sets of chairs stamped with the initials WP beneath a crown. The mark is that of Whitehall Palace, and it has been suggested that the chairs came from there as the Chamberlain's perquisite following the fire of January 1698, when the palace was burnt 'together with exceeding rich furniture of antiquity'.[1] As the Duke had by then ceased to hold the office they could perhaps have been a Royal gift of earlier or later date, or have been acquired following the coronation of William & Mary, when furnishing changes would undoubtedly have taken place. The Duke, incidentally, was

amongst those who invited the Prince of Orange to come to England in 1688, so such marks of the Royal favour were not unlikely.

That foreign workers were active in London is clear from various sources. Frenchmen who were employed by the

[1] *Margaret Jourdain,* Stuart Furniture at Knole, *1952, page 22.*

Court included Jean Poictevin, de Lobel, la Pierre, Pelletier, Pic and Michon, as well as Peter Pavie and Peter Gullibande.[1] The latter was perhaps a relative of John Guilbaud, who made the fall-front cabinet illustrated in Figs. 85 and 86, and affixed to it his label (Fig. 81). The first-noted spelling of the name occurs in the Royal accounts in 1690, recording the supply of two Scriptoires [writing-cabinets] 'inlaid with flowers' at a cost of £15 apiece.

Men of Dutch origin were little less prominent, and included Richard Vanhuissen and Gerreit Jensen, whose name was sometimes anglicised as Johnson. The latter was patronised by John Hervey, later first Earl of Bristol, who made the following entry in his account book on 25th May 1696:

Paid Mr Gerreit Johnson yͤ Cabinett-maker in full of his bill for yͤ black sett of Glass, table & stands, & for yͤ glasses, etc., over yͤ chimneys & elsewhere in dear wife's apartment, £70.

Presumably this 'black' suite was of ebony, a wood fashionable at the time. Johnson, at about the same date, supplied Queen Mary with 'One Ebbine Cabbonete plated with silver and Looking Glass . . . , and stands of ebbone plated with silver and

[1] R. W. Symonds, Furniture-Making in 17th and 18th Century England, 1955, page 108.

Below, Fig. 80: Writing-table veneered with 'fine markatree' of the type executed by the Royal cabinet-maker, Gerreit Johnson, on legs of turned walnut with plain stretchers; the front legs hinging forward to support the flap. Circa 1690; width 94 cm. (Christie's.)

Right, Fig. 81: Label of John Guilbaud, cabinet-maker, at the Crown and Looking-Glass, Long Acre, London. Circa 1695. See also Fig. 85. (H. W. Keil Ltd.)

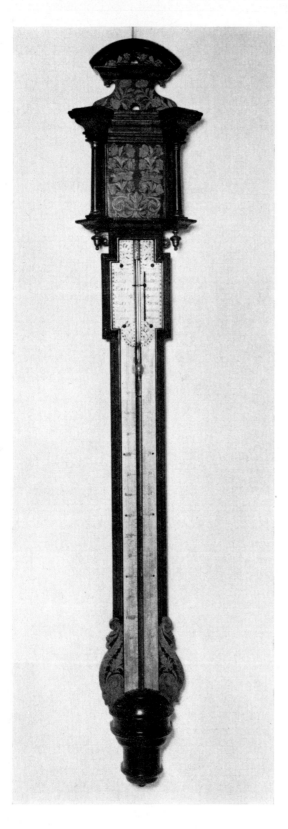

Left, *Fig. 82: Barometer in a marquetry case. No maker's name. C. 1700; height 127 cm. (Bearnes & Waycotts.)* **Right,** *Fig. 83: Cabinet on stand, doors open to display interior fitment of drawers and a small central cupboard, veneered with walnut 'oysters' and raised on legs of turned solid walnut. C. 1680; width about 110 cm. (Mallett & Son Ltd.)*

looking Glass'. He made furniture for use at Kensington Palace as well as for other Royal residences, including a 'fine writing-desk inlaid with metall' which is now at Windsor Castle. His accounts speak of 'fine markatree', and a tall cabinet with glazed doors to the upper part, also now at Windsor, is most probably one supplied by him for Kensington in 1693.[1]

Other entries in John Hervey's *Book of Expenses*, which was printed in 1894, throw a little light on furnishing habits:

1688		
May 2	For a scrutore,	£8
1689		
Oct. 7	For a chest of drawers for yᵉ nursery,	£1
Oct. 11	Paid then to Noul Tirpane a french varnisher in full for 10 chairs, a couch & two taboretts [stools] & all other accounts to this day	£12
Nov.	Due to yᵉ joiner who made the chairs, stools & squabs for my wife,	£19
1690		
Feb. 17	Paid then to Medina yᵉ Jew for a Tea-Table, & 2 pair of china cupps for dear wife,	£10
1691		
Oct. 10	Paid Mrs Hicks for a cradle-skreen,	£1. 6s.
1692		
June 17	ffor yᵉ chest of drawers bought at Stow-Green ffair,	£1. 17. 6d.

The future Earl would seem not to have been averse to buying second-hand furniture. The chest of drawers for £1 would have been very cheap indeed for a new one

---

[1] *Ralph Edwards & Margaret Jourdain,* Georgian Cabinet-Makers, *third edition 1955, pages 35–8, plates 5–8.*

Fig. 84: Frame carved profusely with flowers, fruit, birds, and two winged cupids supporting a crown, at the base a dagger and mace; attributed to Grinling Gibbons, and at one time in the Royal Hospital, Chelsea, designed by Sir Christopher Wren and built between 1682 and 1691. 132×99 cm. (Mary Bellis.)

of any quality, but he may have considered he had spent enough money on the contents of the room after having paid only three days before

> . . . for a silver hanging candlestick for the nursery, weighing 17 ownces, 10 pennyweight, £5. 11s.

The tea-table purchased from Medina may also not have been a new one, as other transactions with him suggest he dealt in second-hand goods. They included: 8 March 1690, 'a parcell of old china for my dear wife, £11'; 13 March 1690, 'a pair of old china rowlwaggons [tall cylindrical vases] for dear wife, £7. 10. 6d.'; and 20 June 1691, 'a Persian carpett (all of silk) to lay under a bed, and an old china Rowl-waggin, 22 guineys'.

It was noted above that John Hervey bought what was probably a suite of ebony furniture from Gerreit Jensen, and the use of other exotic timbers became fashionable at the time for those who could afford their cost. Importations from North and South America vied with others from the Indies, to satisfy a taste for the bizarre that would provide a background for the lavish clothing and conversation of Society. Thus, there was a liking for olive-wood and king-wood, the latter known at the time as 'Princewood' and brought from Brazil.

Veneering invited the employment of any unusually-marked woods that could be placed to show to the best advantage. A growing walnut tree when damaged heals itself by producing a crusted lump termed a 'burr', which, when sliced through, shows innumerable highly decorative tiny black curls. Again, the branches of olive, laburnum and some other trees, when sliced in order to produce round or oval sections, were also highly esteemed. Furniture wholly or partly covered with them is referred to as 'oyster-veneered', in allusion to the superficial likeness of the pieces to the shell of an oyster. Edges of drawers and of flat panels were generally cross-banded: namely, with a narrow straight-grained veneer running inwards from the edge, and often had a line of herring-bone interposed between the cross-banding and the principal surface (Fig. 88).

EBONY was particularly favoured for clock-cases, the movements of which had been greatly improved in reliability after 1660. The grand-father, or long case, was made so that the dial was set conveniently at a height of about six feet (2 m). While the first examples were gracefully tall and narrow-waisted, the body of the case soon broadened to accommodate a wider-swinging pendulum that gave greater accuracy.

The small-sized table- or bracket-clock was also encased in ebony veneered on oak and mounted in gilt brass, while exceptional examples were given mounts of silver which contrasted well with the sombre woodwork.

Both types of clock case also followed current fashion and were veneered with floral marquetry, sometimes covering the entire surface and alternatively in shaped panels reserved on a ground of walnut. While the cases were no doubt at first made by cabinet-makers as part of their normal trade, it is probable that as demand increased they became the work of men specialising in them alone.

The barometer, also brought into wider use through the surge of scientific activity of the period, emerged from the laboratory as a useful adjunct of daily life in about 1680.[1] Its height was regulated by the

---

[1] *Nicholas Goodison*, English Barometers 1680–1860, *1969.*

length of the glass tube of mercury, which had to stand at least 30 inches in height to perform its task of measuring atmospheric pressure. In most instances cases made for them prior to 1700 consist of a straight length of wood with a shaped turned cover at the base to protect and conceal the mercury cistern, and an expanded area at the top to frame the plates and marker. Overall was a neat hood which gave many examples the silhouette of a miniature long-case clock, while many of the surviving specimens have marquetry decoration (Fig. 82). Those of Thomas Tompion, who is probably more renowned for his clocks, are exceptional as regards both shape and the ornamentation of their cases.

The looking-glass was another article that leapt into popularity following the Restoration. Although sheets of mirrored glass were by no means unknown prior to that time, the demand for them greatly increased. They had been made in England for almost a century, but the majority of them, and those most esteemed, were brought from Venice. Copy-letters preserved in the British Museum refer to the activities of two London glass-dealers, John Greene and Michael Measey, active about the year 1670, in this connexion. They sent careful instructions to their supplier, Allesio Morelli, in Murano, telling him to use double-bottomed boxes and to send duplicate invoices to save as much import duty as possible.

By 1676 the second Duke of Buckingham had established a manufactory at Vauxhall; an establishment of which the name endures through being attached, usually without justification, to any sheet of aged-looking mirror-glass. The glasshouse was visited in 1676 by John Evelyn, who noted on 19th September of that year, after seeing a marble-yard at Lambeth:

> We also saw the Duke of Buckingham's glasse-worke, where they made huge vases of metall as cleare, ponderous and thick as crystal [rock-crystal];

also looking-glasses far bigger and better than any that come from Venice.

The sheets were made by what is known as the 'Broad' process, in which a bubble of the molten material was blown and pulled into the shape of a huge sausage. When the elongated mass had reached the desired size, both ends were cut off, a slit made along the remaining tube and it was pressed out flat. It had then to be annealed by slow cooling and was afterwards ground until it was perfectly flat all over. The size of the sheet was limited not only by the manipulative skill and the lung-power of the craftsman, but also by the fact that the more the bubble was enlarged the thinner became its walls. If they were too thin, the sheet

Opposite and below, *Figs. 85 and 86: Writing cabinet, open and closed, veneered with walnut and fitted with gilt metal handles, escutcheons and carrying-handles, by John Guilbaud. Circa 1695; width 109·2 cm. See Fig. 81. (H. W. Keil Ltd.)*

would not withstand the strain of grinding without which it would have been too distorted for use.

Wood frames datable to the last decades of the 17th Century often present a problem as to their original purpose: whether they held a looking-glass or a painting, although in some instances the two were interchangeable. The frames surviving in largest numbers which were certainly used for glasses are of the so-called 'cushion' shape, with a deep rounded moulding and smaller mouldings at the inner and outer edges. It was usually surmounted by a shaped cresting, plain, carved or pierced, and the glass within it was given a scarcely discernible bevel. An impression of just such a frame is seen on John Gilbaud's label (Fig. 81), where it is used to illustrate the fact that his workshop in Long Acre was at the sign of the Crown and Looking-glass.

Frames of various types, especially those very finely carved in wood such as lime, were probably intended for paintings, although many were subsequently transformed into looking-glasses. The elaborate example shown in Fig. 84 is attributed to Grinling Gibbons, the foremost carver of his day. He was born in Rotterdam of English parents, and when 23 years of age was 'discovered' by John Evelyn, who recorded in January 1671 that he found him

> . . . in an obscure place by meere accident as I was walking neere a poor solitary thatched house in a field in our parish [Deptford].

Although the King, to whom Evelyn introduced his work, did not make a purchase, Wren employed him and his merits were soon acclaimed. Gibbons specialised in delicate carving of groups of fruit, flowers and cherubs, and as was said at the time, 'there being nothing in nature so tender and delicate as the flowers and

festoons about it, and yet the worke was very strong'. While much of his employment was to decorate the panelled walls of rooms, as at Petworth, Sussex, and the interiors of churches, as in St. James's,

Fig. 88: Portion of a drawer-front showing (A) principal veneer; (B) herring-bone; (C) cross-banding (D) moulded edge. Walnut, circa 1720.

Piccadilly, he also carved frames. Inevitably, for one who reached the pinnacle of an enduring fame, much more is attributed to his agile chisel than can be substantiated.

The style of much of Gibbons's work was based on that in stone popularised by Inigo Jones, designer of the Banqueting House, Whitehall, amongst numerous other buildings, who died in 1651. Another architect, Daniel Marot, epitomised the design of late 17th-Century furniture in a series of engravings published in 1702 and later (Fig. 87). Marot was a cosmopolitan; born in Paris in about 1662, he was a Protestant and left the country in the year before the revocation of the Edict of Nantes made life there untenable for those of his faith. He went to Holland, where he worked for the Prince of Orange and others, designing furniture and its setting, as well as laying out gardens. Arriving in England in 1694, he is known to have been paid a sum for unspecified work relating to the gardens of Hampton Court Palace four years later. It is thought likely that he also had a part in the furnishing of the palace, and that he provided designs for some of the French craftsmen then working in London. His style shows a mixture of French and Dutch, with the former in the ascendant, and it is agreed that the influence of his engravings was widespread on both sides of the English Channel.

8 : The Orient

As early as 1598 an English translation of Jan Huyghen van Linschoten's volume of travels *Navigatio ac itinerarium*, was printed and published in England. Based largely on his own experiences and in part on what he had been told by other voyagers, he recorded what was known to him of a style of furniture-decoration then unknown in Europe. He wrote of lacquer, with which, he said:

> They cover all kinds of householde stuffe in India as Bedsteddes, chairs, stools, etc., and all their turned wood-worke, which is wonderful common and much used throughout India: the fayrest workemanshippe thereof cometh from China, as may be seene by all things that come from thence, as desks, Targets [?targes: shields], Tables, Cubbordes, Boxes, and a thousand such like things, that are all covered and wrought with Lac of all colours and fashions.

Lady Arundell's ownership in 1641 of 'a little black Indian table' and other pieces was referred to earlier (page 52), and it was suggested that they might have been Chinese in view of the prevalent loose use of the term Indian. This was applied equally to produce of that land, and to objects brought from anywhere in the East in ships of the East India Company, either English or Dutch.

It is not until the reign of Charles II that references to lacquered furniture in English ownership become at all frequent, and diaries and documents begin to note the existence of examples in the more fashionable homes. Just three days prior to the coronation, Samuel Pepys saw at the residence of James, Duke of York, 'two very fine chests, covered with gold and Indian varnish, given him by the East Indy Company of Holland'.[1]

While on a visit to Lord Wotton, at Belsize House, Hampstead, in June 1676, John Evelyn noted:

> The furniture is very particular for Indian cabinets, porcelane, and other solid and noble moveables.

Again, three years later, at a mansion in St. James's, although having a low opinion of the owner, he admired his possessions, and entered in his diary:

> I din'd together with Lord Ossorie and the E. of Chesterfield, at the Portugal Ambass[rs], now newly come, at Cleveland House, a noble palace, too good for that infamous. . . . The staircase is sumptuous, and the gallerie and garden, but above all y[e] costly furniture

---

[1] *On 20th April 1661. The Duke of York later reigned as James II.*

belonging to the Ambassador, especially the rich Japan cabinets, of which I think there were a dozen.[1]

The English, Dutch and Portuguese were rivals in bringing goods from the Orient. The two first-named founded trading Companies in the first years of the 17th Century, but with the preoccupations of the Civil War the English effort slackened. After some years of indecision, Cromwell's government finally decided to renew the Company's charter, and in 1657 this was done: reviving the original monopoly, with permission to fortify and plant in any of its settlements. As a result, stock was offered for sale on the open market, and the public eagerly subscribed a total of £739,782.[2]

The amount was much greater than could be employed, and the Company took up only about half of it. Encouraged in such a manner, it rapidly regained its former vitality and thenceforward flourished. It was assisted not only by the support of the public, who looked for good dividends on their capital, but by a more liberal Parliamentary policy respecting the export of coin and bullion. This had been argued as being gravely detrimental to the national interest, but was defended stoutly by Sir Dudley Digges, who if nothing else was a painstakingly precise calculator of pounds, shillings and pence, Sir Dudley, a judge and a diplomatist, was authorised to present the Company's case and in his Defence of Trade, published in 1615, he wrote:

> The importation of East India Commodities had broken the monopoly of the Hollanders; had saved the nation

£69,666. 13s. 4d. and had cheapened the articles.

The patriotic argument, that if the trade was allowed to lapse the Dutch would take it all and drive the English completely out of the East, was a strong one. Returning

Opposite, *Plate 15: Cabinet painted in gold with Oriental subjects on a red ground, the stand and cornice of wood covered in gilt gesso. Early 18th Century; width about 110 cm. See also Plate 16. (Pelham Galleries Ltd., London.)*

Below, *Fig. 89: Cabinet decorated with Oriental figures in landscapes on a black ground, the gilt stand carved at the corners with cherubs' heads and the frieze centred on a standing figure. Circa 1685; width about 137 cm. (The Vyne, Hampshire: The National Trust. Photograph The Connoisseur.)*

---

[1] *On 4th December 1697. Evelyn seems to have had an unhappy time, as he wrote of the meal: 'the dishes were trifling, hash'd and condited [seasoned] after their way, not at all fit for an English stomach, which is for solid meate. There was yet good fowle, but roasted to coale, nor were the sweetmeates good.'*

[2] *S. A. Khan, East India Trade in the Seventeenth Century, Oxford, 1923, page 90.*

travellers were reported as bringing back tales of the cruelties inflicted by the Dutch on anyone trading wherever it was considered they were interlopers.

The bulk of trading by the Companies centred on India and the nearby islands and the East Indies, and the principal cargoes sought were spices, drugs, textiles of various kinds, and saltpetre: the latter was a constituent of gunpowder, ever in brisk demand somewhere in the civilised world. Decorative articles in the form of furniture and porcelain formed only a small proportion of imports, and in London the directors of the Company showed only slight interest in the commercial possibilities of what were then little more than amusing trifles from strange and distant lands. In 1659, however, two of their ships returned from having ventured as far as Canton; although precise details of their cargoes are unrecorded, they may well have included some of the lacquered goods likely to have been for sale in the port.

Lacquer has been described as 'a sort of gummy juice which drains out of the bodies and limbs of trees', and comes, in fact, from the *Rhus vernicifera*, which is called by the Chinese *chi sui*.[1] An anonymous report given in London to the members of the Royal Society in the late 17th Century gives details of the way in which the substance was obtained and used:

> Lack is the Sap or Juice of a Tree which runs out slowly by Cutting the Tree, and is catch'd by Pots fasten'd to the Tree; 'tis of the Colour and Substance of Cream; the Top, that is Expos'd to the Air, immediately turns Black, and the way they make it Black and fit for Use, is to put a small Quantity into a Bowl, and stir it continually with a piece of Smooth Iron for 24 or 30 Hours, which will both Thicken it and make it

Opposite, *Fig. 90: Bureau-cabinet decorated with shaped panels of figures in landscapes in gold on a black ground, the doors inset with looking-glass and the double-domed cornice deeply moulded. Circa 1710; width 101·5 cm. (Phillips, Son & Neale.)* **Above,** *Fig. 91: Cabinet decorated with Oriental scenes on a black ground, the stand and cornice of carved and pierced gilt wood. Circa 1690; width 105·4 cm. (Temple Newsam House: Leeds City Art Gallery.)*

Black; to which they put a quantity of very fine Powder of any sort of Burnt Boughs, and Mix it very well together, and then with a Brush lay it Smooth on any thing they design to Lack, then let it Dry very well in the Sun, which will then be Harder than the Board it is laid on; when it is thoroughly Dry you must Rub it with a Smooth Stone and Water till it is as Smooth as Glass, . . .

It was then said erroneously that a coat of turpentine-based varnish was applied, clear for black lacquer or coloured to choice, but in fact the lac itself was stained prior to use. After decoration the varnish was employed to protect the gilt design, which was finished with careful polishing.

[1] *Margaret Jourdain & R. Soame Jenyns*, Chinese Export Art, *1950 (reprinted 1968), page 17. The first chapter of the book is entitled 'Lacquer and Lacquered Furniture'.*

The same observer mentions a disability affecting many who did the work or merely watched others doing it:

> The Swelling that often happens to those that Work the Lacker'd Ware, and sometimes to those that Pass only by the Shops and look on them at Work, is from the Lack, and not the Varnish. . . .[1]

There appear to be no reports of those who bought the decorated furniture being similarly affected.

The lacquer had to be applied in thin coats, 'not too slowly, not too quickly' in the words of a Chinese writer, each being allowed to dry thoroughly before the next was added. Up to thirty-six layers were recommended for certain types of work,

[1] *John Lowthorp*, The Philosophical Transactions . . . Abridg'd, *3 vols., 1705, vol. III, page 619. Methods varied in details from craftsman to craftsman.*

and the final surface was polished carefully 'to bring it to a gloss'. There was a variety of colours to be had, but black was the most popular choice; perhaps because it was fashionable, but possibly it was selected because it may have been cheaper than any other. Various shades of red, green and brown have been recorded, but in most instances time has caused fading and deterioration. The present-day external appearance of most examples is not always an indication of what they were like three centuries ago; only when they have been

Opposite, Fig. 92: Bureau-cabinet decorated with panels of floral patterns in gold on black reserved on an aventurine (gold-sprinkled) ground. Early 18th Century; width 54·5 cm. (Sotheby's.) **Below,** Fig. 93: Twelve-fold draught screen of Chinese incised (Coromandel or Bantam) lacquer; the central design depicting buildings and figures. Circa 1700; height 283 cm. (Bearnes & Waycotts.)

Left and right, *Figs. 94 and 95: Bureau-cabinet decorated with scenes in gold on a black ground, the upper part with double doors surmounted by a swan-neck pediment, the base containing three long drawers with shaped fronts, and the sides with carrying handles. A document preserved with the cabinet reads: 'Sept. 13th, 1740. In the forenoon of this day my Chinese lacquer cabinet was delivered by the Carier [sic] at my house in Abingdon. It was procured by my dear friend John Folgham in Pekin for the sum of £200 Sterling & was brought to England in the bark* Marie Celeste *being on the sea for many months. It looks vastly elegant in the Parlour and adds distinction to the room. Thomas Flight.' The latter was the father of the Thomas Flight who bought the Worcester porcelain manufactory in 1783, and Folgham was perhaps a relative (? father) of John Folgham who traded as a cabinet- and case-maker in London during the second half of the 18th Century. Height 239 cm.*

fortuitously kept from light and dirt, namely the interiors of some cabinets, is the true original beauty to be seen.

The types of finished work can be divided into four categories: flat and decorated in colours and gold and silver; partly raised and similarly decorated; incised, with the edges of the cuts emphasised in colours and gold; and inlaid with designs in jade, ivory, mother-of-pearl and other materials, painted and gilt.

The incised variety has for long been known as Bantam or Coromandel, from those places in the East Indies and India, respectively, where the Dutch had depots. Its making differed from that of the other types, and would have been the work of specialists. A layer of sand was applied to the wood surface; this was followed by some fine clay, a stratum of grass-fibre and a further coating of clay. The work was then polished and lacquered, cut and coloured,

and after further polishing, it was complete. Often, sheets of rice-paper were included in the composition, and assisted in binding the whole together so that when incised it was less likely to crack and break away.

THE appeal of the finished product to Europeans was two-fold: its durable and attractive surface, and the decoration with which the latter was embellished. This had not only a brilliance of colour and gilding, but most people were intrigued by the Oriental draughtsmanship with its unfamiliar subjects and naive lack of perspective.

Not only had the work been brought some thousands of miles, but on it were scenes of a fairy-tale world and its peoples. This happy domain, known as Cathay, was one of snow-capped peaks on which there grew a stranger flora and sported a more curious fauna than could be imagined by anyone in

the West. The humans living in that distant land, it has been said,

> are small and neat. Hats, shoes and cheekbones are worn high, while moustaches, pigtails, and finger-nails are encouraged to grow to inordinate length.[1]

Furniture depicting such beings in such surroundings could not fail to enchant when it reached the workaday chill of Europe; a continent where, on the whole, despots did not spend their waking hours

Below, Fig. 96: Cabinet of black lacquer, the decoration incised and coloured. Early 18th Century; width about 100 cm. (Christie's.) Opposite, Fig. 97: Looking-glass framed in pieces cut from an imported screen of incised lacquer of the type shown in Fig. 93. Circa 1685; width 99 cm. (Victoria and Albert Museum.)

composing odes, or select their officials according to their proficiency as poets.

While the subjects of most of the scenes would have been known to the Chinese as deriving from their extensive mythology, an inhabitant of London, Paris or Amsterdam would be ignorant on the point. The Eight Horses of Mu Wang would not have been seen as the legendary steeds of the Chou sovereign, but merely as a group of playful ponies, and the goddess Kwan Yin as nothing more than a heathen idol. The River Spirit out riding in his chariot may perhaps have been in the mind of John Milton when he wrote of

> Sericana [the land of silk] where Chinese drive
> With sails and wind their cany wagons light.

While much of the imported furniture was in the form of cabinets, the doors enclosing sets of drawers of different sizes, and great chests with rising lids, a large proportion comprised folding screens. By the end of the century the cargoes were varied in content, although many of the items were small and expendable and few, if any, survive. A list of the goods carried in three ships which reached port in 1700 included drugs, tea, textiles, chinaware and so forth, as well as the following, all of which were described as 'lacquer'd':

Sticks for fans	£13,470
Trunks, escretors, bowls, cups, dishes, etc.	10,500
Tables inlaid	189
Panels in frames, painted and carved for rooms	47
Boards	178
Brushes	3,099
Tables not inlaid	277
Fans for fire	174
Boards for screens	54[2]

[1] *Hugh Honour,* Chinoiserie: A Vision of Cathay, *1961, page 6.*

[2] *Esther Singleton,* Dutch and Flemish Furniture, *1907, quoted by Francis Lenygon, op. cit., page 272, footnote.*

Left, Fig. 98: Looking-glass framed in panels of rolled paper (filigree) work within borders of black and gold japanning surmounted by a shaped and pierced cresting. Circa 1685; width 47 cm. (Victoria and Albert Museum.) Above, Fig. 99: Table-top of black lacquer inlaid in mother-of-pearl with a scene of galloping horsemen. Early 18th Century; 50·7 × 87·6 cm. (Saltram, Devon: The National Trust.)

The folding screens stood between two and nine feet in height, and had up to a dozen leaves of a width ranging from 18 inches to two feet. Their decoration, either painted or incised, was usually arranged as a central panel within a border covering the entire article, so that each single leaf bore a portion of the whole. The principal subjects were landscapes, always mountainous both with and without horsemen, or bird's-eye views of buildings with people in their gardens and courtyards.

While many of the screens have survived intact, more were dismembered as soon as they reached the hands of a cabinet-maker. In most instances the leaves were patterned on both sides, and by carefully sawing them in two a double supply of veneer was obtained. It was glued in the same manner as any other veneer to English-made chests of drawers and cupboards, and to the frames of looking-glasses. The fact that the treatment almost invariably destroyed the composition was of secondary importance at the time, but to more discerning eyes the results are little less than ludicrous. Typical is the frame in Fig. 97, on which the designs on the two horizontal members are each composed of unrelated fragments arranged on their sides, and in neither case do the patterns at the corners blend with those on the uprights. The shaped cresting has also been assembled from odd pieces, but with a less obvious sequel.

The lacquer-work executed in Japan differed from that of China, and enjoyed a high esteem in the latter country and farther afield. The instructions given to the London East India Company's agents in the 1690's continually stressed that any goods sent home should be 'better and cheaper'. In 1697 the Captain of the *Trumball* at Amoy was told to return with 'all sorts of useful things in fine Japan lacquer but bring little or no ordinary lacquer ware', and two years later another instruction included the words 'none of the wares are to be sent but what are lacquered in Japan'.[1]

Contacts between Europe and Japan had first been made by the Portuguese, whose missionary, Francis Xavier, landed there in 1549. During the ensuing months, with the aid of a smattering of the local tongue but mostly with the use of Portuguese and Latin, which were of course completely

incomprehensible to his listeners, he managed to gain several hundred converts to Christianity. There was also a certain amount of two-way trading, especially in guns, which the Japanese had never seen before and which they quickly realised were great assets in conducting their perpetual internal wars.

The Portuguese continued to come and go,

Below, *Fig. 100: Table decorated with carved and gilt gesso, the top of Chinese black lacquer inlaid in mother-of-pearl. (See Fig. 99.) Early 18th Century; width 87.6 cm. (Saltram, Devon: The National Trust.)* **Right**, *Plate 16: Another view of the cabinet shown in Plate 15, with the doors opened. (Pelham Galleries Ltd., London.)*

---

[1] *M. Jourdain and R. Soame Jenyns, op. cit., pages 69 and 23.*

building churches and acquiring congregations to fill them, but in 1593 the Jesuits found that some Spanish Dominicans and Franciscans had arrived from Manila and were competing with them for souls. The rivalry was intensified by the coming in 1600 of a Dutch vessel, the *Liefde*, which was followed by other vessels, and in 1609 the Dutch, 'the Red-haired Barbarians', were permitted to set up a headquarters on the island of Hirado, where they were joined in 1613 by the English. The Portuguese and Spaniards, and their religion, were completely banned; the English gave up trading after ten years, having lost money in the venture, but the Dutch persisted in the face of immense difficulties and reaped their reward. They had a virtual monopoly of trade with Japan during their 31 years on Hirado and a further two centuries on the tiny island of Deshima, to which they were strictly confined from 1640. Thus any Japanese lacquer reaching the West during almost the entire 17th Century was, with few exceptions, brought thither by the Dutch.

The Japanese favoured black grounds for their work, often decorated with gilding only but sometimes with the addition of raised work. In most cases ornamentation was more restrained than that of the Chinese, and comparatively large areas of background supported small, well-drawn scenes. Similar subjects were popular in both countries; mountainous landscapes with flowers and animals, but only very rarely including figures.

Most Japanese lacquering was done on small articles, and prior to 1859, when the country was opened to the world, the quality of workmanship was extremely high. Two-door cabinets like those of China were also made but can be identified with little experience. It is unusual to find that Japanese work was mutilated in England, as were the Chinese screens. In France, however, it was not uncommon, and in the 18th Century eminent Parisian cabinet-makers incorporated panels of Japanese lacquer in their furniture to great effect. On a miniature scale, the same was done by some of the makers of snuff-boxes, who mounted tiny panels in chased gold set with precious stones.

Although the Company in London specified 'Japan laquer' this may well have been no more than a generic term for good quality articles of any origin, notably Chinese. The public were uninformed as well as careless about such details, and as the Orient was so far away it probably seemed a triviality. A parallel is recorded by a mid-18th-Century Swedish ship's chaplain, Peter Osbeck, who visited Canton in 1751. He wrote:

> The Cantonese take great pains to make their goods strike the eye, and sell well; but they do not take the same care to make them good and strong; nor do they offer them as the best and finest; for when they have a mind to praise their goods, they say that they come from Nanking, viz. Nanking silk, Nanking ink, Nanking fans, and even Nanking hams.[1]

Thus, it is clear that verbal confusion was common to East and West.

---

[1] *Peter Osbeck*, A Voyage to China and the East Indies, *2 vols., 1771, vol. II, page 244. This is a translation by J. R. Forster of a work published in Stockholm in 1757.*

9: The Pseudo-Orient

WHILE those at home were completely enchanted with Oriental workmanship and its products, one English traveller made no bones about his dissatisfaction.

Fig. 101: Folding-top card table of padouk-wood inlaid with engraved mother-of-pearl, made in the East in the English style of c. 1730. Mid-late 18th Century; width 83·8 cm. (Saltram House, Devon: The National Trust.)

Captain William Dampier, who combined in his person the divergent roles of hydrographer and buccaneer, was in the Far East in the late 1680's and some years later published an account of his various voyages. Among his comments on China he wrote:

> The Joyners in this country may not compare their work with that which the Europeans make; and in laying on the Lack upon good or fine joyned work, they frequently spoil the joynts, edges, or corners of Drawers of cabinets. Besides our fashions of Utensills differ mightily from theirs.

Steps were taken to satisfy a demand for 'Utensills' more agreeable to European tastes, and it was said that as early as 1670 'some artisans were sent out to introduce patterns for sale at home'. Further, at least one 'ingenious joyner' is recorded as having travelled to the East, along with a supply of suitable timber, in an effort to obtain for the home market exactly what was required as regards types of articles, their construction and their finish.

The successful trading of the English East India Company inevitably led to criticism. The country had to contend not only with imports of furniture but with much larger consignments of textiles, and on top of these there was a continual influx of Huguenot workers. A broadsheet of the time summed up what was in many minds:

Plate 17: Armchair decorated in gold and colours on a red ground, by Giles Grendey (1693–1780). Circa 1730; height 113 cm. (Temple Newsam House: Leeds City Art Gallery; photograph H. Blairman & Sons, London.)

> The Loom, the Comb, the Spinning Wheel,
> Do all support this kingdom's Weal.
> If you will wear your own silk and woollen,
> You will keep your coin, your poor, your bullion.[1]

Despite the writer's obvious lack of poetic instinct, the sentiment is plain and the oft-repeated cry of the protectionist unmistakable.

One of the most virulent and vocal of such men was Prince Butler, who penned a number of pamphlets lashing the Company and listing the views of its more extreme critics. 'Had not', he inquired,

> a hundred thousand poor rather come to their Parishes for want of work, and all the land of England fall two years' purchase, than that the Cookmaids should not be cloathed in India Silks and the ladies in Calicoes? . . . Would it not be better if we send for the corn to the East Indies, for theirs is much cheaper than ours? And employ the Dutch Shipping, for they always sail much cheaper than we do, and then we may send our own ships to all foreign nations that either want or hire them?[2]

Another pamphleteer broadened the panorama of imminent disaster by writing thus of the unsuspecting Asians:

> As they have already almost swallowed and engrossed the Silk weaving, Throwing, and Fan-making of England, brought all our Cabinet-making into contempt; they will by the same ways and means ruin all Trades and Manufacturies. . . . Their plenty of Copper and Tin will give them opportunity to ruin both our Braziers, and Pewterers, Tin-men and Mines. The Joyners and Carvers they have pretty well encroached upon.[3]

While some of this dismay and abuse was motivated by a genuine fear of unemployment and bankruptcy, most was the result of sheer jealousy. The Company was doing well, but its ample profits, gained at great risk, were shared only among the fortunate few enjoying the monopoly of supplying a clamorous market. In print and in Parliament the argument was prolonged, while the ships sailed back and forth in increasing numbers.

The London furniture-makers were at first powerless to compete with lacquer; it was a hitherto unknown substance that was no less mystifying than porcelain. Their only weapon at first was a political one, and the Joiners' Company did its utmost to inspire the Government to prohibit imports. This was no more successful in the case of furniture than it was with other Far Eastern goods, and before long they learned to face up to the competition. The successive arrivals of larger and larger consignments soon made buyers selective, and while they were less fastidious than Dampier they became discontented with only Oriental articles to choose from. To fill this demand for English styles of cabinets and so forth, London-made pieces were shipped out to China, given their lacquer covering and then re-shipped home. Less laborious and time-consuming was the alternative of dispatching English craftsmen, whose task was to instruct the Chinese wood-workers in what was required. Not unpredictably, the London joiners saw this as an even greater threat to their livelihood, and strongly deprecated the sending not only of their fellow-men, but of 'models and Patterns of all sorts of Cabinet goods to the East'.

As true lac was unobtainable in the West, the only course left open to those in England was to produce an acceptable imitation. This they did by the use of varnishes,

---

[1] *Khan, op. cit., page 222.*

[2] *Ibid., page 225.*

[3] *Ibid., page 224, footnote 2.*

which lacked the unique quality of the prototype but resulted in a passable copy. The same might be said of the draughtsmanship of those who drew the Chinese-style figures and landscapes, which did no more than approximate to the real thing.

It is known that as early as 1616 an Englishman who was then in Rome wrote to the Earl of Arundel, requesting employment and stating that he had 'bene emploied for the Cardinalles and other Princes of these parts in worke after the China fashion wch is much affected heere'. More than seventy years were to pass before the 'secrets' of Western simulations were made public in England. In 1688 John Stalker and George Parker, of whom otherwise very little is known, published a book on the subject, of which the title-page clearly set forth at length the contents in these words:

A Treatise of Japanning and Varnishing, Being a compleat Discovery of those Arts. With The best way of making all sorts of Varnish for Japan, Wood, Prints or Pictures. The Method of guilding, burnishing and lackering, with the Art of Guilding, Separating, and Refining Metals: and of Painting Mezzo-tinto-Prints. Also Rules for Counterfeiting Tortoise-shell, and Marble, and for Staining or Dying Wood, Ivory, and Horn. Together with Above an Hundred distinct Patterns for Japan-work, in Imitation of the Indians, for *Tables*, *Stands*, *Frames*, *Cabinets*, *Boxes*, &c. Curiously Engraven on 24 large Copper-Plates. By John Stalker, and George Parker. Oxford, Printed for, and sold by the Authors, *John Stalker*, at the Golden Ball in *St. James's* Market, *London;* or by *George Parker*, at Mr. *Richard Woods* House over against the *Theater* in *Oxford*. In the Year MDCLXXXVIII.[1]

Slightly later in date came John Salmon's *Polygraphice*, which was a compilation of instructions for those who wished to follow the twin arts of painting and alchemy; to many minds perhaps a curious pair to find within the same covers. First issued in 1672, by 1701 the eighth edition

[1] *Reprinted with an introduction by H. D. Molesworth, 1960.*

Left, *Fig. 102: Drawer-front from the interior of the cabinet in Fig. 104, showing a hunting scene and 'Oriental' flora and fauna.*

Above, *Fig. 103: Another drawer-front from the same cabinet; in both instances the facial features and costume of the figures represent a compromise between European and Oriental.*

had swollen to two volumes with a total of 940 pages. Salmon's chapters on japanning drew heavily on Stalker and Parker, and enumerated in detail both materials and methods that were essential for good results. The twenty requisite instruments and utensils include Dutch rushes ('which are to be had at the Ironmongers in Foster-lane') for rubbing-down, bottles and funnels, and two or three hundred mussel-shells ('middle-sized Horse Muscle-shells are fittest for these Occasions') for use in mixing colours.

For the actual varnish or japan he gave receipts for ordinary varieties which contained shellac, dragon's blood (a red-coloured resin) and saffron, and the best kind which was based on seed lac. The work was to be prepared by coating it with whiting and size,

> and so often repeat this till you have hid all your Hollownesses, Crevises, Pores and Grain of your Wood, letting it throughly dry between every Laying.

The final layer is smoothed with rushes, and given two coats of seed lac varnish,

a day or two after Varnish it over with Black, or what other Color you design, according as has been directed; and when sufficiently dry, you may finish it by Polishing it.

Salmon gives an interesting list of the different colours in which the work might be finished. They are as follows:

Black: Incorporating lamp-black—'It is made by the burning of Lamps, having many Wicks, covered with a very large Top, at a due distance, to receive the Smoak, which continually sticking upon this Top, produces this black Color'.

White: the ground laid with whiting and size and then given two coats of starch and water; a very clear varnish is applied, but this yellows with age and the work gradually acquires a deep creamy tinge.

Blue: made with additions of white lead and smalt; the latter a powdered blue glass.

Red: made with vermillion.

Dark red: the above, plus powdered dragon's blood.

Pale red: vermillion with the addition of white lead.

Olive: 'English Pink in fine Pouder' with some lamp black and raw umber.
Chestnut: with Indian red and a little white lead.
Lapis Lazuli: much as for blue, above, but then 'run straglingly over all your Piece, in wild irregular Streaks (as a resemblance of Nature) with Liquid or Shell-Gold, filling the Blew as you see occasion. . . .'.

He also lists several alternative methods for simulating tortoiseshell and marble.

For the actual designs Salmon gives brief instructions for copying drawn or engraved versions, which are to be rubbed on the back with chalk:

> Then lay this Paper, Draught, or Print, upon your varnisht Table or Box, with the whited side next to it, and upon the very same place where you design the Draught should be made, and with a piece of small Wire, or a Needle fixed in a small Wooden Handle, round (not sharp Pointed) which is called a Tracing Pencil, go over, and Trace as much of the Print as you see convenient.

Raised work was added if required, with a mixture of whiting and gum, and various kinds of gold or near-gold were recommended for the ornamentation. They were mixed with gold-size or gum-water, having a final coat of clear varnish to preserve them from wear and tear. The finished effect, according to Stalker and Parker, having a surface that will 'glissen and reflects your face like a mirror'.

In 1688 it was noted that Bantam or Coromandel work was then out of fashion:

> . . . tis now almost obsolete, and out of fashion, out of use and neglected. . . . I think no person is fond of it, or gives it house-room, except some who have new Cabinets out of old Skreens made. . .[1]

This did not prevent either Stalker and Parker or Salmon giving details of how the work was to be done. The woodwork had to be coated with the whiting mixture to a depth of a quarter of an inch, and the design was cut with great care 'for the wood itself ought not to be touched with the Graver'.

Opposite, *Fig. 104: Cabinet decorated with figures and birds in a landscape in gold on a black ground. Late 17th Century; width 104·7 cm. (Saltram House, Devon: The National Trust.)*

Below, *Fig. 105: Bureau-cabinet decorated with Oriental scenes in gold and colours on a red ground; a label on the back printed with the inscription: 'Made by John Belchier at the Sun in St. Paul's Church Yard'. Circa 1730; width 122 cm. (Christie's.)*

---

[1] *Stalker and Parker, 1960 edition, page 37.*

Below and opposite, *Figs. 106, 107: Two views of a bureau-cabinet decorated in gold and colours on a sealing-wax red ground, the mirrored doors surmounted by a moulded serpentine pediment topped by pierced brackets and gilt vase finials. Circa 1700; width about 122 cm. (Mallett & Son Ltd.)*

The complexities of japanning did not daunt amateurs, and in their *Treatise* the authors refer to 'those whiffling, impotent fellows, who pretend to teach young Ladies that Art, in which they themselves have need to be instructed, and to the disgrace of the Title lurk and shelter themselves under the notion of Japanners, Painters, Guilders, &c.'. Some schools for the genteel included such subjects in their curriculum, and in 1689 Sir Ralph Verney wrote to his daughter 'who had a desire to jappan', agreeing to satisfy it by paying a fee of one guinea and £2 for the necessary 'materials to work upon'. These last words point to the availability to amateurs of articles especially for the purpose, and it seems not improbable that that they may have been already lacquered leaving the final ornamentation to the discretion and skill of the buyer. The fact that the preparation and application of the ground was the most important and exacting part of the process, requiring time, patience and experience for success, suggests that there may have been a good demand for semi-finished pieces.

The amateurs increased in numbers during the first decades of the Eighteenth Century, and among them the name of Mrs Delany stands out. Not only was she a skilled practitioner at all kinds of elegant handiwork, but her surviving correspondence provides evidence of the activities of both herself and her friends. Thus, in September 1729 she wrote from London to her sister:

Everybody is mad about japan work; I hope to be a dab at it by the time I see you.

Later in the year, to the same correspondent, she mentioned visiting a Mrs Barnes who lived somewhere in the capital

. . . where I saw nothing extraordinary but the fine japan you so much despised; it put me in mind of the fine ladies of our age—it delighted my eyes, but gave no pleasure to my understanding.

Two years later, once more to her sister, she wrote of a friend's possession:

> You never saw such perfection as Mrs Clayton's trunk; other's Japan is beautiful, but this is *beauty*—it is the admiration of the whole town.

Although it has been suggested that ready-prepared articles may have been offered for sale, Mrs Delany eschewed such short cuts. On Christmas Day 1729 she wrote:

> I am going to do little boxes for a toilette. I will send you [her sister] a box and some varnish; but as to laying the ground I doubt you will find it difficult unless I could show you the way, which I hope next summer to accomplish.

She was a determined woman, and one cannot doubt that the instruction was given while regretting that the results have not been preserved.

Indeed, although a good quantity of japanned furniture has survived from the first decades of the century the major proportion of it has perished for one reason or another. A brief paragraph in a newspaper, *The London Journal* of 7 January 1720, makes it clear that the amateurs were indeed following fashion and that there was no diminution of supplies from the Orient:

> On Monday last, at the Conclusion of the Sale of Lacquered Wares at the East India House, that, with the former Sale, amounted to One Million: and the next Day they began the Sale of China Wares.

Some modern writers have differentiated between Oriental work and European by referring to the former as *lacquer* and the latter as *japan*. However, clear-cut distinctions are seldom observable, for there are further sub-divisions between work executed in England and that done in France, Holland and Italy. In all of those countries there was a similar copying of Far Eastern ornamentation, and while much of it betrays a Western hand it is less

easy in many instances to name its nationality.

Over the years there has been much transfer of movables from one country to another, as travel for both people and goods has become less difficult. This has further complicated the position with regard to European work, and once the original home of an example has been forgotten it can rarely be named with certainty. Although the characteristics of the japanning varied only insignificantly from one land to another, the shaping of the furniture is sometimes revealing. For example, bureau-cabinets and chests of drawers were usually given more noticeably curved outlines in Holland than they were in England, and this is visible just as much in japanned pieces as it is in those of walnut. Other features, such as details of construction are also helpful.

The Chinese and Japanese did not normally use dovetailed joints, but under the tuition of foreigners it is not unlikely that they learned to do so. A simple joint will probably indicate a Far Eastern maker, but the reverse is not a reliable guide. More significant is the presence of Chinese characters on the back of a drawer, with a similar marking on the carcass to show where it belongs. A comparable example occurs with the chair illustrated in Plate 18, one of a set, of which each loose seat is inscribed (Fig. 112) to ensure it is correctly placed in the frame for which it was made.

Some authorities state that it is generally the draughtsmanship of the designs that enables work to be recognised as of Eastern or Western origin. This is true enough, and the facial features of figures, when any are present, can reveal the truth as in Fig. 102. However, the nature of true lacquer, its hardness and extremely smooth surface are not usually difficult to tell apart from the simulations of 'foreign devils', whose coloured varnishes rarely withstand the ravages of time with success.

The English fondness for lacquer and

Below, *Fig. 112: Detail of lacquered chair in Plate 18. The materials and method of upholstering are not European, where nailed broad, flat webbing would have been used in place of threaded rope and matting. The wood frame of the loose seat is marked with Chinese characters (see top and bottom of picture) coinciding with similar markings on the chair itself, to ensure that the correct seat is placed in each chair.*

Right, *Plate 18: Chair, made and decorated in China, with gold designs on a dark blue ground. Early 18th Century; height 110·5 cm. (Private Collection.)*

japan had begun to abate by the mid-Eighteenth Century, when Chinese influence on furnishings started to take other forms. It did not disappear altogether, but never again became as widespread as in those days when the *Vision of Cathay* was fresh. The Twentieth Century has seen a revival of the taste when in the 1920's japanned work enjoyed a sudden and brief renaissance. Not only were new articles then made to meet the demand, but much old and innocently plain furniture was transformed.

In 1923 a London firm advertised that it

> . . . will be pleased to submit estimates for the decoration of rooms in either modern or antique lacquer . . . or will undertake to lacquer single pieces of furniture, Bedroom suites, etc. . . . a chair can be lacquered in black and gold, red and gold or blue and gold lacquer and decorated in Chinese style from 15*s*.

They further pointed out that

Below, *Fig. 113: A vase of flowers in the Oriental manner, from Stalker and Parker's* Treatise, *1688.*

. . . nothing looks so out of place as a modern piano or pianola in a room furnished in antiques and the only method of making it harmonise with the old furniture is to lacquer it in the Chinese style of Charles II, William-and-Mary or Queen Anne.

This firm was not the only one active at the time, and later, and much of their work now passes unsuspected as genuine. Many a longcase clock dating from about 1720, the genuine oak surface deceptively coloured and gilt and with nearly half-a-century of wear and tear, is accepted as being of the period throughout.

Much of the imported furniture was made from locally-grown timbers such as padouk, which flourished in Burma and the Andaman Island. At Goa, in Java and elsewhere the Portuguese and Dutch set the natives to work copying European pieces to be shipped home for sale (Fig. 101). Padouk is a well-marked, close-grained wood, which is noticeably heavy in the hand. Unlacquered furniture made from it reveals its origin not only by its distinctive appearance but by its weight in comparison with an article of similar bulk made in the West.

10 : William Kent

THE majority of the lacquered or japanned cabinets discussed and illustrated in previous chapters are raised on elaborately designed stands; the cabinet and its support vying with each other for attention. Made of wood, gilded or silvered, the stands may be seen as a survival of the earlier custom of mounting precious objects in gold, silver-gilt or silver. This was especially current during the Sixteenth Century, when Chinese porcelain was first brought to Europe and fortunate recipients of specimens treated them in the manner of diamonds and rubies.

The process of gilding wood was known to the ancient Egyptians and in 1437 was recorded by Cennino Cennini, Italian author of a treatise on the techniques of the arts: *Il Libro dell'Arte*. It was employed sparingly in England until the Restoration, thereafter holding a place, which varied in importance from time to time, in the decoration of all kinds of furniture.

In their *Treatise* of 1688 Stalker and Parker give details of the process employed at the time, which differed little from that of the servants of the Pharoahs or that in the manuscript of Cennino. They state at the outset:

> Guilding accepts not of base materials, is wholly unacquainted with dross or allay, and the finest unadulterate gold is the only welcom and acceptable guest.

Then follow precise instructions for the two types of work: oil-gilding and water-gilding.

The former was used principally, but not exclusively, for outside purposes, being both cheaper and more enduring than the other. Apart from these two considerations it has a different finished effect because it cannot be burnished and made to shine. It is an exaggeration to state that ''twill appear with a dazling and unusual lustre, and its beauty will be so durable, so well fortified against the injuries of wind and weather, that the attempts of many Ages will not be able to deface it'.

Wood suitable for intricate carving was too soft to provide a satisfactory surface for water-gilding. It was necessary, therefore, to coat it with a layer of *gesso* so that the article would present a smooth and firm exterior. The word, from the Italian, signifies a mixture of size and whiting, the former being made thus:

> Take two pounds of the cuttings and shavings of clean Parchment; the Scriveners vend it for 3d. the pound: wash and put it into a gallon of fair water, boil it to a Jelly, then strain, and suffer it to cool, and you will find it a strong Size.

The size was mixed with a quantity of whiting and the composition was brushed on, so that 'the Whiting may enter into every private corner and hollowness' of the

carving. It was allowed to dry and the process was repeated several times, 'never forgetting this caution, to grant a through-drying time between every turn by the fire or Sun'. After a sufficient thickness had been applied the whole was smoothed with rushes or a piece of fish-skin.

The sharpness of the carving, by then somewhat blurred, had to be restored by careful re-cutting or, in other words:

> . . . with an instrument called a Gouge, no broader than a straw, open the veins of the Carved work, which your Whiting has choakt and stopt up.

The adhesive used to make the gold fast to the gesso was also made with some of the size. Different conditions demanded variations in the ingredients and, no doubt, experience was essential, for

. . . 'tis a difficult task to find the true quantity of each distinct thing that is required to make up the composition; and the reason of it is this, because you are compelled to vary and alter the proportions, as each season changes its qualities of moisture and dryth; for the Summer demands a stronger Size than the Winter.

Opposite, *Plate 19: Chair of carved beechwood, gessoed and gilt, the top rail carved with the crest of Sir William Humphreys Bart., whose arms were granted in 1717; the back and seat covered in contemporary Genoa velvet. Circa 1717; height 121·9 cm. (Victoria and Albert Museum.)*

Below, *Fig. 114: Pair of chairs decorated with carved and gilt gesso, the knees with lions' masks holding rings. Circa 1735. (Christie's.)*

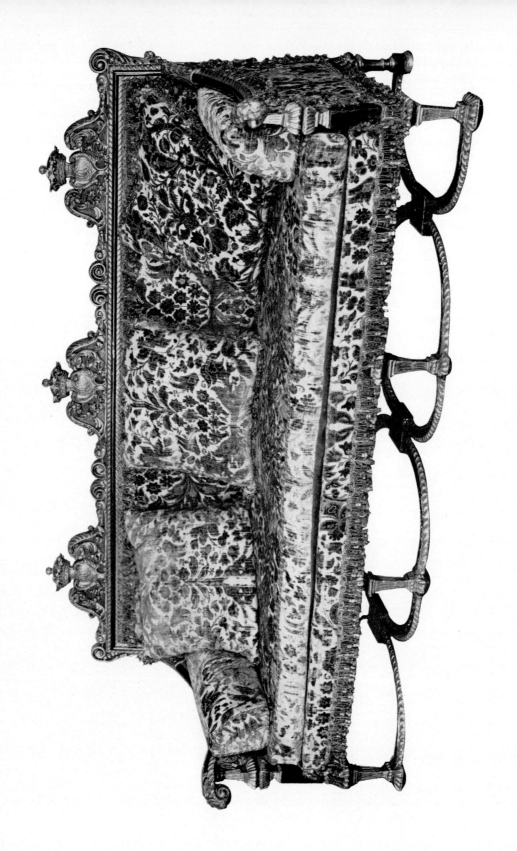

Figs. 115, 116: Settee and day-bed, the frames of carved and gilt wood surmounted by coronets over the cypher of Thomas Osborne, first Duke of Leeds (1631–1712), of Hornby Castle, Yorkshire. Circa 1695: lengths, settee 213 cm., day-bed 157·5 cm. (Temple Newsam House, Yorkshire: Leeds City Art Gallery.)

Fig. 117: Two-door cabinet overlaid with metal panels decorated with Oriental scenes in gold on a black ground; supported on a stand carved with two cherubs amid flowers and leafy scrolls. Late 17th Century; width 101·6 cm. (John Keil Ltd., London.)

Having tempered the size to the season, the mixture was prepared by adding to it fine pipe-clay or Armenian bole (known also as Armoniak); the latter an earth obtained from Armenia and called nowadays gilder's red clay. It was augmented by what Stalker and Parker referred to as 'a small bit of candle-grease', or alternatively a little beeswax or tallow. Slightly warmed and of a thin consistency, it was brushed on so as to cover every part of the work.

The gold was, and still is, used in the form of leaves measuring about 4 inches (about 10 cm.) square, made from pure or alloyed metal beaten to extreme thinness. In 1621 it was said that an ounce of gold could be made to cover an area of 105 square feet, nearly a century later the French scientist, Réaumur, increased the figure to 146½ square feet, and as much as 300 square feet has since been claimed. The degree of malleability is dependent on the presence or absence of alloying metals, these being added in part to lower the cost but principally to influence the colour. It can range from red through yellow and green to white, by the admixture of suitable proportions of copper and silver.

The metal is alloyed to produce the required tint, cast and cut into small pieces, each of which is then repeatedly hammered and re-cut until it is thin enough. The beating is performed with the metal placed between sheets of goldbeater's skin: a strong membrane obtained from ox gut.

To apply the leaf, the prepared surface was moistened piecemeal with a watery brush over an area of about a square foot at a time, and the leaves laid on. They were placed singly on a small cushion and picked up with a pad of cotton-wool, a brush or a squirrel's tail which was breathed on to make the leaf adhere. Then it was placed carefully on the sticky size and pressed into position.

A knife was used to cut leaves to size on the cushion

> . . . as your work calls for them, for your own interest contriving how you may bestow 'em without waste, which is the principal concernment a Guilder ought to be vigilant and circumspect in; and that darling-metal, which we foolish Mortals covet, nay almost adore, is certainly too pretious to be lavishly consumed, and unprofitably puff'd away.[1]

After the whole area had been covered it was left to dry. In due course, if all had been performed correctly, the projecting parts could be burnished with the aid of a dog's tooth or an agate pebble, leaving them glittering in contrast to the untouched matt background.

Similarly, oil-gilding could be applied over gesso, but might also be used directly on the surfaces of unprepared wood or metal. The adhesive medium was a size based on dried linseed oil (known as fat oil), which was mixed with ochre and other ingredients so that it was both slow-drying and waterproof. Like water-based size it was painted on, but required no further treatment except to allow it time to become tacky. As soon as it had reached this state, the leaves were applied in the same manner as before. While oil-gilding was longer-lasting, the drawback to it was that it could not be burnished and its decorative uses were thereby limited.

Silver could also be beaten into leaves, but not to the extreme thinness of gold. It was employed occasionally on furniture and more frequently on leather; in the latter

[1] *This and preceding quotations are from Stalker and Parker, op. cit., 1960 edition, pages 53 and 57–59.*

instance particularly on the Cordova variety which has painted and apparently gilded decoration. Silver leaf was found to tarnish, so the finished work was given a coat of varnish to seal it from the atmosphere. Often, as in the instance of leather, the varnish would be stained yellow, so that the result was a close resemblance to gilding achieved at a much lower cost.

Carved articles were sometimes left with a smooth matt background, but two other treatments became popular during the Eighteenth Century. In the early decades it was common to give the flat surfaces a random pattern of tiny circles, applied with a punch which was tapped carefully so as not to crack and mar the gesso. The individual circles averaged no more than $\frac{3}{16}$ of an inch (4 mm.) in diameter and often

Fig. 118: Pair of dining chairs with upholstered seats and backs, the cabriole legs covered with carved and gilt gesso. Circa 1735. (Parke-Bernet Galleries Inc., New York.)

comprised two concentric rings. Use was also made of a sanded ground, executed by mixing ordinary sand, fine or coarse, with the gesso and gilding it in the normal manner. It is frequently found on the inner mounts of picture frames or in the borders of looking-glass frames, and was mostly confined to comparatively small areas.

In the past, when family mourning was treated with considerable outward display, the principal rooms of a house were hung with black. In the case of gilt-framed looking-glasses it was not uncommon on such occasions to cover the frames with black paint, and up to some few years ago it was not uncommon to find them remaining in this condition. With infinite patience it was usually possible to chip away the hardened paint with the edge of a copper coin (a silver one with a milled edge would mark the surface), and so uncover the original gilding. On occasions it was found that it had been painted when the gold was already getting worn, but sometimes this had not occurred and it was revealed in its pristine state.

The skill and consequent fame of Grinling Gibbons undoubtedly influenced many craftsmen, most of whom made use of the motifs favoured by the master. Acanthus leaves, winged cherubs' heads and swags of fruit and flowers were draped about and between gently curving table- and cabinet-legs, the frieze being of sufficient depth to make a cross-stretcher superfluous. Although some were made of lime-wood, they were more commonly of pine or fir, and a small proportion of surviving specimens are painted rather than gilded. This may have been done to avoid expense or else to suit a personal taste.

Some of the cabinets, whether imported or home-produced, were also given a shaped pediment, which improved their appearance by lessening their manifestly box-like form. Carved and gilded to match the base, they were affixed along the top, but in most instances they have been destroyed. Being easily removable they were especially liable to be mislaid and damaged, and to find one in place today is unusual (Plates 15 and 16).

By the end of the Seventeenth Century the stands, like tables, followed the styles popularised by Daniel Marot, with a shallow frieze and straight legs linked by elaborate stretchers. The acanthus leaf and other features remained largely unaltered except that the cherubs were replaced by adult male and female masks, and there is a close resemblance to articles then being made across the English Channel in Paris.

A different type of carved ornamentation made an appearance early in the Eighteenth Century. The general form of a stand or table became simplified, the legs were curved gracefully and the frieze was reduced to a wide moulding, while the gesso itself, in place of the wood, received the majority of the chiselling. The raised portions of the design were burnished and stood out brightly from the ground, which was usually punched, and the effect when new must have rivalled the work of the goldsmith. The years have taken a very heavy toll of such pieces, which were comparatively lightly constructed and of which the depth of the exposed decorative surface was to be measured in thousandths of an inch. Few specimens retain their original gilding, and modern replacements of it are fashionably given a 'distressed' finish, perhaps in an effort to allay suspicions that it might be new.

The rise to prominence of the architect William Kent was responsible for the use of gilding on a grandiose scale. Horace Walpole discussed him 'with equal impartiality on the merits and faults . . . the former of which exceedingly preponderated', and wrote:

He was a painter, an architect, and the father of modern gardening. In the first character, he was below mediocrity; in the second, he was a restorer of the science; in the last, an original,

and the inventor of an art that realizes painting, and improves nature. . . . His portraits bore little resemblance to the persons that sat for them; and the colouring was worse, more raw and undetermined, than that of the most errant journeyman to the profession. . . To compensate for his bad paintings, he had an excellent taste for ornaments, and gave designs for most of the furniture at Houghton, as he did for several other persons. Yet, chaste as these ornaments were, they were often unmeasurably ponderous.[1]

Kent was employed by royalty and the nobility, and some of his work still remains at Kensington Palace and Houghton Hall, the latter executed for Sir Robert Walpole, of whose five children Horace Walpole was the youngest, while the furniture he designed for Devonshire House, Piccadilly, and Chiswick House is now at Chatsworth. He died in 1748, by which time he held a number of posts in the Office of Works and was Inspector of Paintings in the Royal Palaces as well as Portrait Painter to the

Above, *Fig. 119: A table for Sir Robert Walpole at Houghton Hall, Norfolk, pen and ink and wash drawing by William Kent, dated November 1731. 15·5 by 28·5 cm. (Victoria and Albert Museum.)* **Right,** *Fig. 120: Mahogany bureau-cabinet, the upper part carved and the door inset with looking-glass, designed in the manner associated with William Kent. Circa 1735; width 109·2 cm. (Christie's.)*

King, in the last of which roles George II did not call upon him to exercise his much-criticised talents. His activities as a designer of furniture were confined in the main to the years 1720 to 1740, and while his own output in the direction was limited he had numerous imitators.

Walpole pointed out that the Earl of Burlington, an amateur architect, designer of Chiswick House and Kent's unfailing patron, had given the interior 'too many correspondent doors in spaces so contracted; chimneys between windows, and, which is worse, windows between chimneys'. This excessive regularity of appearance is to be noticed in many interiors of the time, and a further feature, noted by the same writer,

[1] *H. Walpole*, Anecdotes of Painting in England, *edited by R. N. Wornum, 3 vols., 1876, vol. iii, pages 57–8.*

is the 'constant introduction of pediments and the members of architecture over doors and within rooms'. With this treatment, the inside walls of a room closely resembled the exterior as regards architectural features.

The size of the principal rooms in most of the mansions then being built called for movables on an equal scale, and the treatment of their ornament had to be no less generous. The piers, or flat spaces between the evenly-placed windows invited a fresh approach which gave rise to the provision of tables over which were hung looking-glasses of matching design.

Kent's chairs have a heavy, throne-like appearance which makes it clear that their purpose was ornamental rather than functional. The example illustrated in Fig. 121 closely resembles a set of four armchairs designed in the early 1730's for Chiswick House and now at Chatsworth. It is assumed to have belonged at one time to the first or second Marquess of Hertford, whose descendants formed what is now the Wallace Collection, but when or whence they may have acquired the chair is unrecorded. Its design shows a use of Italian motifs, and is a reminder that Kent spent most of the years between 1709 and 1719 in that country, returning to his native land with a collection of prints and plaster casts which, he wrote from Rome in 1718, 'will be of great use to me when I cannot see ye Antiques'.

During his lifetime William Kent's reputation was largely confined to his clientele, many of whom were related to one another, and to his acquaintances. He was overshadowed, perhaps knowingly, by the cultured and well-connected Burlington, and subsequently it has been no easy task to discover in every instance whether some or all of the credit belongs to the nobleman or to his protégé. Confirmation of his obscurity in the public eye may be seen in the terse announcement of his death printed in the pages of the *Gentleman's Magazine* for April 1748 (Vol. XVIII, page 187):

> 12. Wm. Kent, Esq; a commissioner of the board of works, of mortification in his bowel.

The foremost cabinet-maker of the time was Benjamin Goodison, who advertised from his premises at the Golden Spread Eagle, in Long Acre, from 1727. He was cabinet-maker to George II as well as to his son, Frederick Louis, the Prince of Wales, and examples of his work are extant at Buckingham Palace and Hampton Court. Kent designed in 1732 a highly ornamented barge for the Prince, and for the latter's

fourth son, Prince Henry Frederick, later Duke of Cumberland, a cradle. The barge, which was rowed by twenty-one dashingly-uniformed oarsmen, is now in the Victoria and Albert Museum. When the Prince of Wales, father of the future George III, died in 1751, it was Goodison who embalmed the body and supplied a coffin for it, and draped the principal rooms of the royal residence, Leicester House, Leicester Square, with black fabric.[1]

Benjamin Goodison worked also for other distinguished patrons, amongst whom were Thomas Coke, first Earl of Leicester, who built Holkham Hall, Norfolk, and the Duke of Newcastle, who owned both Claremont, in Surrey, and Newcastle House, in Lincoln's Inn Fields, London. William Kent designed Holkham and is known to have worked for the Duke, and as both Kent and Goodison held Royal appointments they were doubtless acquainted. Further, as some of the latter's identified work is in the style popularised by the architect it is tempting to conclude that they collaborated in those houses and perhaps elsewhere.

In addition, Goodison's contemporary, James Moore the Younger, son of the James Moore who was a partner of John Gumley, is known to have worked to Kent's designs.[2]

---

[1] *Averyl Edwards*, Frederick Louis, Prince of Wales, *1947, page 184.*

[2] *Christopher Gilbert, 'James Moore the Younger and William Kent at Sherborne House' in the* Burlington Magazine, *March, 1969.*

Fig. 123: Design for a settee and alternative cresting, from Some Designs of Mr. Inigo Jones and Mr. William Kent, *by John Vardy, London, 1744. See Fig. 122.*

A pair of settees at Temple Newsam House, Leeds, from a suite of which the remainder is now scattered in various collections on both sides of the Atlantic, correspond closely to one of William Kent's published works (Figs. 121 and 123). The settees and other pieces were supplied to Sir John Dutton, of Sherborne House, Gloucestershire, for a

building in the grounds, known as 'The Lodge', used for picnics and parties. Payment for them was made in 1731, and the account-book entry reads:

> To Mr Moore for 2 Mahogany Settees for yᵉ Dining Room at yᵉ Lodge Carved 30. 0. 0.

The furniture known to have been designed by Kent, and that of his copyists, has been censured in modern times. The architect Sir Reginald Blomfield wrote of him that he 'was one of those generally accomplished persons who can do everything up to a certain point, and nothing well. . . . His designs for furniture and the handicrafts in general were about equally inappropriate'. These are hard words, but it has to be remembered that Kent's work was exclusively to the order of wealthy patrons and mostly for houses that are, especially by later standards, of enormous size. In their original settings his tables, chairs and other pieces are not misplaced, but form an integral part of a monument to the first English professional architect to design both a house and its contents. Torn from its environment, in the words of Margaret Jourdain, 'it loses much of its effect'.[1]

---

[1] *Margaret Jourdain*, The Works of William Kent, *1948. See also H. M. Colvin*, A Biographical Dictionary of English Architects, *1954.*

11 : Looking-Glasses

THE widespread popularity of looking-glasses was mentioned when discussing other types of furniture that became current during the years following the Restoration. The glasses were employed in two prominent positions: over the fire-place, or between windows. In the former they would reflect rooms and their contents, between windows their tall and narrow shape conveniently filled an awkward space, while in either situation they increased the existing illumination. Not least, they were useful for personal appraisement.

While the distinctive pier-glass had its shape dictated by the expanse of wall against which it was to be hung, that of the overmantel was less rigidly defined. It was often rectangular and of a length to match that of the mantelpiece, and no taller than was essential. Examples of this style, known commonly as overmantel glasses because they would fit nowhere else, began to be made in about the year 1700.

Surviving specimens betray the difficulty experienced in obtaining large sheets of glass, and invariably comprise two small-sized pieces flanking a larger central one.

The latter was often given an arched or otherwise-shaped top, and the whole bordered by narrow strips of mirrored glass or of glass decorated from the back in gold and colours (*verre églomisé*). Occasionally the borders were cut with simple scallops or, more ambitiously, with floral motifs and small figures. Visible woodwork was kept to an absolute minimum and if present took the form of gilt mouldings seldom more than a finger in width.

The same observations apply to pier-glasses of the time, which were also composed of several sheets of glass, according to their height. These were frequently three in number, the uppermost being shaped, and again the border was of glass.

Of this last type there were a number on the premises of Gerreit Jensen at the time he gave up business. An advertisement in *The Daily Courant* on 2nd May 1715, read:

On Thursday the 12th instant, the Goods of Mr. Johnson, Cabinet-Maker to her late Majesty Queen Anne, having left off Trade, at his House in St. Martin's Lane, upon the Pavements, near Long-Acre; consisting of several very large

Looking-Glasses in Glass Frames, and other Glasses, Chimney-Glasses and Sconces, Right India Japan Cabinets and Tables, Book-Cases, Chests of Drawers, Buroes, a fine Shandeleer, and a large Ebboney Book-Case finely Carved, and all Sorts of Cabinet-Makers Ware.[1]

Some extant examples are in the mansions for which they were originally made, and bear the crests or coats of arms of their owners. A number of looking-glasses with his coronet and crest or monogram on them were supplied in 1711 to the Earl of Nottingham and are still at Burley-on-the-Hill, Rutlandshire. They were made by Thomas Howcraft and Richard Robinson, of London, and the bills detailing the charges of the two men, as well as correspondence concerning transport of the goods, have been preserved. They were despatched the 100 miles by wagon and horses, and the driver made it clear that he would accept no responsibility if the vehicle overturned during the journey and his load sustained damage.

Two very large-sized looking-glasses are in the State Bedroom at Chatsworth, Derbyshire. Rectangular in shape, within two borders of clear and sapphire-blue glass, the principal plate is surmounted by a shaped glass cresting, in one instance centred on the arms of the first Duke of Devonshire, in the other on the Garter star. The first of them bears a name and date scratched on it: 'John Gumley 1703', and a reference to them dated that year shows that they cost £200.[2]

John Gumley was a successful cabinet-maker and glass-dealer, who was in business between about 1694 and 1729 and of whose career there is a fair amount of information.

[1] Quoted by Francis Thompson, 'The Work of Gerritt Jensen at Chatsworth' in The Connoisseur, vol. XCVI, page 192 (October, 1935).

[2] R. Edwards and M. Jourdain, Georgian Cabinet-Makers, third edition 1955, page 41, plates 14 and 15.

Opposite, *Plate 21: Gilt wood table with marble top, from a design in Thomas Langley's* The City and Country Builder's and Workman's Treasury of Designs, *1740, copied in turn from one by the Frenchman, Nicholas Pineau. Width 178 cm. Pair of carved and gilt chairs. All c. 1740. (Victoria and Albert Museum.)*

Below, *Fig. 124: Pier glass, the frame carved and gilt gesso. Circa 1720; height 160 cm.*

Not only did he make a fortune in his lifetime, but his daughter married into the nobility to become the wife of William Pulteney, Earl of Bath. It may be mentioned that she was described by a contemporary as lacking 'any one good agreable quality but beauty'. Further, she gained herself the distinction of a mention in verse, albeit an admonitory one, from the pen of Alexander Pope. In a short piece entitled 'The Looking Glass' he wrote of her:

> With scornful mien, and various toss of air,
> Fantastic, vain, and insolently fair,
> Grandeur intoxicates her giddy brain,
> She looks ambition, and she moves disdain.

He then apostrophises her for having forsaken the qualities she possessed when single, and adds:

> O could the sire, renown'd in glass, produce
> One faithful mirror for his daughter's use!
> Wherein she might her haughty errors trace,
> And by reflection learn to mend her face:
> The wonted sweetness to her form restore,
> Be what she was, and charm mankind once more!

Anna Maria Gumley's appearance in print was paralleled by that of her father, who was the subject of notices, in considerably more flattering terms, by Sir Richard Steele. In both *The Spectator* and *The Lover*, in 1712 and 1715, respectively, Steele commended Gumley and his glass to his readers, and on the second occasion drew their attention to his newly-opened premises in the Strand.

In the latter publication[1] he wrote in characteristic style:

---

[1] The Lover, to which is added The Reader, *May 13, 1715.*

Opposite, *Fig. 125: Pier glass, the border cut and engraved and the shaped upper plate cut in a pattern of flutes.* Circa 1710; height about 160 cm.

I shall now give an Account of my passing yesterday Morning, an Hour before Dinner, in a Place where People may go and be very well entertained, whether they have, or have not, good Taste. They will certainly be well pleased, for they will have unavoidable Opportunities of seeing what they most like, in the most various and agreeable Shapes and Positions, I mean their dear Selves. The Place I am going to mention is Mr. *Gumley's* Glass-Gallery over the *New Exchange.* . . . No imagination can work up a more pleasing Assemblage of beautiful things, to set off each other, than are here actually laid together. . .

He also mentions 'my honest Friend and polite Director of Artificers, Mr. Gumley . . .'.

The New Exchange, which was known also as Exeter Exchange, had been erected in 1678 and occupied a site on the north side of the Strand between Wellington Street and Burleigh Street. It was fitted up in the manner of a market or bazaar, with small booths for the sale of hosiery, millinery and so forth, on the ground floor. John Gumley leased an upper floor in 1714, where he displayed furniture of all kinds as well as looking-glasses.

His display was visited soon after Steele's eulogy had appeared, by Dudley Ryder; a young man who was destined to become Attorney-General and who died suddenly in 1756 only two years after his promotion to Lord Chief Justice. On Thursday, November 3rd 1715 he recorded in his diary:

> Went into the glass warehouse over the New Exchange. There is indeed a noble collection of looking-glass, the finest I believe in Europe. I could not as I passed by there help observing myself, particularly my manner of

Below, *Fig. 126: Carved and gilt gesso, the cresting in the form of a pierced shell. Circa 1725; height 122 cm. (Christie's.)*

walking, and that pleased me very well, for I thought I did it with a very genteel and becoming air.[1]

Ryder was 24 at the time, so his preoccupation with his personal appearance is understandable, and in any event his diary was written for the laudable purpose of self-study and certainly not for publication. In the century of James Boswell the philosophers' advice 'Know thyself' was taken with great seriousness.

In 1687 the second Duke of Buckingham died; he had done most things in the course of his lifetime and these included founding the Vauxhall glass-house. For some years following his demise there were no public notices of the enterprise, but it is assumed that it continued trading. Then, in February 1700 an announcement appeared in a newspaper, *The Post Man*, which stated:

> Large Looking-glass Plates, the like never made in England before, both for size and goodness, are now made at the old Glass House at Foxhall, known by the name of the Duke of Buckingham's House. Where all persons may be furnished with rough plates from the smallest sizes to those of six foot in length, and proportionable breadth, at reasonable rates.

A German visitor to England, Zacharias Conrad von Uffenbach, was in Vauxhall ten years later and noted seeing a pottery there at work. 'Next', he recorded,

> we went into the glass or mirror hut near by, where, fortunately, they happened just then to be blowing.

He described the process in use (see page 109), and after mentioning that the sheets of

---

[1] The Diary of Dudley Ryder, *ed. W. Matthews, 1939, pages 130/1.*

glass were annealed over a period of three days, concluded:

> Then the panes are sold to other people who cut and mount them, making mirrors of them; this is a special trade followed by many people in London.[1]

Earlier, in 1691, at the Bear-Garden, Bankside, a new glass-house had been opened for the manufacture of window-glass but a few years later it had widened its activities. In 1702 a notice in *The Post Man* informed readers that they might obtain there

> . . . Looking-Glass Plates, Blown from the smallest size upwards, to 90 inches, with proportionable breadth, of lively Colours, free from Veins and foulness, incident to large Plates that have been sold hitherto.

A further competitor came on the scene in 1705, when John Gumley, hitherto solely a cabinet-maker, joined with some other men in opening a glass-house at Lambeth, a district adjoining Vauxhall. Its output was confined to plates suitable for looking-glass, and it was not long before the new company was involved in petitions to Parliament as well as a pamphlet war.

Gumley alleged that the Bankside concern was trying to create a monopoly and force up prices, and at the same time that they 'refus'd to sell any Glass-Plates to Persons they thought were Enemies to their Monopoly, unless they would give Twenty Pounds per cent more than they were sold for to others . . .'.

The arguments died away after Parliament refused to suppress the Lambeth or

---

[1] London in 1710, from the Travels of Z. C. von Uffenbach, *translated and edited by W. H. Quarrell and Margaret Mare, 1934, page 132.*

Below, *Fig. 127: The frame with scroll corners, carved with leaf motifs on a punched ground, and the cresting a stylised shell.* Circa *1730; height 117 cm.*

any other newly-started glass-making enterprise, and Gumley's name, in partnership with James Moore, of St. Giles's, is to be found in the Royal accounts between 1714 and 1725 as a supplier of looking-glasses and other furnishings. A pier-glass at Hampton

Below, *Fig. 128: The frame decorated with carved and gilt gesso, and the swan-neck pediment centred on a cartouche. Circa 1730; height 173 cm. (Bearnes and Waycotts.)* **Opposite,** *Fig. 129: Of architectural type, the frieze centred on a female mask and the pediment on a cartouche. Circa 1735; height about 160 cm.*

Court has the central plate bordered by narrow glass with carved and gilt Corinthian capitals at each side, the shaped top being flanked by flambeaux in urns and centring on a female mask with a feathered head-dress. The side-glasses are each divided by a narrow strip of gilt wood, on one of which is carved the name GUMLEY.[1]

John Gumley's will was quoted by R. W. Symonds in *Country Life* (February 27, 1942, page 406), and in it he bequeathed to his mother, Mrs Elizabeth Gumley, the 'Goods and Stock-in-Trade at his Glass Warehouse at the New Exchange in the Strand'. In 1729, in company with William Turing, of Bedford Street, Mrs Gumley supplied a quantity of furniture for St. James's and Kensington palaces, but the Comptroller of the Great Wardrobe was dissatisfied with it and 'thought there might reasonably be abated out of their bill, which amounted to £512 12s. the sum of £361 10s. 6d.'. Further, the Master was advised that the two 'were no longer to be employed as tradesmen for the Wardrobe on account of their notorious impositions'.

A brief notice of a death in the *Gentleman's Magazine* for July 1735 (vol. V, page 387) may refer to the lady in question, and if so she might be excused her lapse from grace on account of age. It runs:

> Mrs Gumley, aged 92, who kept the great China-Warehouse in Exeter Change, about 15 Years ago.

ABOUT 1720 a change in the style of looking-glass frames began to be seen. The outer border of glass was less often present, and the frame itself increased in width to compensate. Also, the shaped glass cresting made way for one of wood, while all the woodwork was given a coat of

---

[1] *R. Edwards and M. Jourdain, op. cit., page 116, and plates 16 and 12.*

gesso which was finished with water-gilding suitably burnished.

At first the new type of frame was given a flat lower edge of similar width to the sides, but gradually it was deepened to achieve a balance of design with the top. When this had occurred it became general to fit the majority of the bases with a pair of scrolled brass candle-holders, so that when the candles were lit their flickerings were attractively reflected from the glass. Most of

these were lost or discarded in the course of time, so all that now remains of them are the two shaped flat-topped pads to which were screwed the small cups holding the arms.

Some large pier-glasses were made in this style (an example with a flat base is illustrated in Fig. 124). The majority of surviving specimens of 1720–30 are smaller, with an average height of about 45 inches (114 cm.).

Designers and makers of the period showed much ingenuity in making use of fashionable motifs. The acanthus leaf is seldom absent, and the eagle, entire or head only, which was to be popular for a long time to come, was an innovation. The central feature, if not an eagle, varies

Left, Fig. 130: One of a pair of looking-glasses, the frame veneered with mahogany and enriched with carved gilt wood, the swan-neck pediment centred on a male mask. Circa 1745; height 140 cm. (Private Collection.) **Below,** *Fig. 131: Two designs for looking-glass frames from* The Gentlemens or Builders Companion, *by William Jones, London, 1739.*

between a formal cartouche, which is named after a roll of parchment or paper, and a shell; the latter being treated in numerous ways so that at times it is indistinguishable from a plume of feathers. More rarely the ornament is a shield with the first owner's coat of arms and a surmounting crest, which can be of value sometimes in deciding the date of manufacture.

Below, *Fig. 132: Frame veneered with walnut and with applied gilt carving, the cresting in the form of an eagle with outstretched wings.* Circa 1750; height about 122 cm. **Opposite,** *Fig. 133: The pair to the looking-glass in Fig. 130, note that the pediment is centred on a female mask.* Circa 1745; height 140 cm. (*Private Collection.*)

Triple-plate overmantel glasses were made with glass borders, sometimes of simple rectangular shape but also with projecting 'wings' at both ends; the latter carved with leaves and scrolls burnished on a matt or punched ground. More imposing and intended to occupy the same position in a room, are others of similar type to the foregoing with an oil-painting above the glass and a continuous frame enclosing both.

The use of gilding for looking-glass frames remained general until about 1735–1740, its long popularity doubtless due to the attractive appearance of silvered glass contrasting with gold. Cost or fashion caused the gilding to take a secondary, but still important, place when walnut veneer began to be used for the major area. Usually on oak, the walnut was selected for its markings, and although this played its decorative part, the skilful outlining of the frame in scrolls and serpentine curves was also a factor. Gilding was confined to a narrow slip bordering the glass, to a central shell or other feature in the cresting, and often to swags of flowers or fruit and leaves down at each side.

The influence of William Kent, with his 'introduction of pediments and the members of architecture over doors and within rooms', is to be seen in the design of frames published by William Jones. As an architect he was responsible for the famous Rotunda in the Ranelagh pleasure gardens, and three years before this was opened he issued a book. Its title is self-explanatory, as were most of them in the 18th Century:

> The Gentlemens or Builders Companion containing variety of useful designs for doors, gateways, peers, pavilions, temples, chimney-pieces, slab tables, pier-glasses, or tabernacle frames, ceiling pieces, &c.

It contained a score of designs for tables and frames (Fig. 131), all of which are sober versions of Kent's more imaginative work.

Equally architectural in inspiration and Kentian in appearance is the looking-glass illustrated in Fig. 134. It is one of a number that have been recorded, each differing slightly from the other.[1] Located during

Below, *Fig. 134: The glass flanked by Corinthian columns and the swan-neck pediment centred on a vase. Probably Dublin.* Circa *1730; height about 200 cm.*

the present century in homes and shops in England, it has not been doubted that they originated there in about 1730–40. Recently, one of comparable style has been found bearing on the back the label of a Dublin firm, and as others, more or less matching but lacking labels, exist in Ireland the entire group would seem to have been made in that country. Like other furniture, their true identity was lost after crossing the sea. It is probable that the mirrored glass used in them came from France, for there is no record of any having been made in Ireland in the Eighteenth Century. Although it might have been sent from England, supplies were always short there, and the French product was considered to be superior.

It has been suggested that people in the past indulged more in narcissism than the inhabitants of the 20th-Century world. No doubt the message of Kipling's lines would have been just as plain then as when he wrote them, although it may be thought that no 17th- or 18th-Century poet would have escaped censure for the rhyme:

> The cruel looking-glass that will never show a lass
> As comely or as kindly or as young as what she was!

---

[1] *G. Wills*, English Looking-Glasses, *1965, plates 52 and 53.*

Right, *Plate 22: Looking-glass in a carved and gilt frame, the cresting centred on a female mask.* Circa *1735; height 165 cm. (Stourhead, Wiltshire: The National Trust.)*

12 : 'Queen Anne Walnut' Bureaux, Writing-Tables

THE early decades of the 18th Century were the years during which were built and furnished not only great mansions, but

Opposite, *Fig. 135: Bureau-cabinet veneered and cross-banded with walnut, the doors inset with looking glass and surmounted by a gabled moulded pediment. Circa 1700; width 103 cm, height 231 cm. (Sotheby's.)* **Below,** *Fig. 136: Veneered walnut bureau-cabinet, the interior fitted with drawers, cupboards and divisions, and the arched doors surmounted by a moulded pediment inset with a shaped panel of looking glass. Early 18th Century; width 104 cm. (Sotheby's.)*

many smaller houses. Thousands of them still stand, one or more in most of the old towns of the British Isles, and they do so despite the march of progress in the form of ever-increasing taxation and the thunder and filth of diesel-engined vehicles. Their rooms were, and remain, eminently suited in size and shape to everyday living, and their internal arrangements, on the whole, are no less convenient than their façades are attractive.

In such houses the extravagantly carved and gilded chairs and tables, so appropriately sited in the rich settings of Holkham and Houghton, were completely alien. A different style of furniture evolved for the purpose; furniture invariably described as 'Queen Anne', which is a generic term for pieces made between the commencement of her reign in 1702 and the end of that of George I in 1727.

In the late 17th Century immigrant workers from France and the Netherlands brought with them new methods of construction as well as styles of ornament different from any hitherto known in England. With modifications to suit local skill and taste they were accepted, and quickly became, in most instances, recognisably different from their prototypes. Furniture based on the engravings of Daniel Marot was highly fashionable in and about the year 1700, but there then began to appear in

Opposite, *Plate 23: Bureau-cabinet with domed top, the door inset with looking-glass. Circa 1720; width 61 cm. (Private collection.)*

some quarters a liking for greater simplicity. It cannot now be decided whether this antipathy towards the florid was engendered by aesthetic considerations or by a lack of money to pay for inlay, carving and gold leaf. Perhaps a combination of both may have been the cause

Queen Anne, daughter of James II and sister of her predecessor on the throne, Mary, was crowned in 1702. It has been said that her piety together with an equally strict parsimony was allied with an indifference towards the Arts, and that this spread from the Court outwards. Her childhood was not a happy one; her adult life, following marriage in 1683 to Prince George of Denmark, was marred by the birth of children who died young; and her tenure of the throne was made irksome by the political intrigues of Whigs and Tories.

Whether the Queen's character actually did affect the tastes of her subjects and induce them to live in more modest surroundings than might otherwise have been the case, is a debatable point. Be that as it may, later generations have had cause to be grateful for the restrained design of so much of the furniture of her reign and of that made in the succeeding decade or so.

Most of the articles are of the simplest forms, relying for their effect on understatement rather than on any ornateness. They owe their charm to carefully-selected veneers, and to craftsmanship that has withstood the rigours of succeeding centuries.

Its lack of sophistication has resulted in little being known about the majority of its makers, and the earlier historians of English furniture did not even mention its existence.

The first to publish pictures and information about such pieces was the late Robert W. Symonds, whose book *The Present State of Old English Furniture* was first published in 1921 and re-issued six years later with its 116 illustrations at 21*s*. More detailed consideration was given to the subject by the same writer in his *English Furniture from Charles II to George II*, published in a limited edition in 1929.

The 260 illustrations in this book were from pieces in the collection formed by Percival Griffiths, who wrote a Foreword to the volume which opened as follows:

> I first began to collect old furniture thirty years ago. At that date, furniture collectors were few and far between, and old furniture shops were correspondingly scarce. The wealthy collector in those days would have nothing to do with English furniture; he interested himself in the more precious products of the Continent—in French furniture, *cinquecento* bronzes, Limoges enamels, and snuff boxes.
>
> One outstanding pecularity of this pre-war [pre-1914] period of collecting was that walnut furniture was a drug on the market, and only oak, satinwood and mahogany were appreciated. Times have now changed, and it is walnut and mahogany that the present-day collector seeks for and admires. I must confess that I have moved with the times, and consequently missed many an opportunity of acquiring magnificent pieces of walnut furniture when nobody wanted them, but which to-day are eagerly sought after, and are becoming increasingly scarce and correspondingly costly.
>
> Walnut pieces that to-day run into four figures could have been easily purchased in 1910 for £80 or £100. This is no exaggeration, as I could name several examples of walnut furniture which were sold at Christie's at about that date and, on reappearing in the

market in recent years, have realised more than ten times their original auction price.

The rescue of 'Queen Anne Walnut' from the limbo of cellars and attics is due to Griffiths and Symonds, who recognised and publicised its qualities. That it is so suited to the proportions of many modern homes has ensured its continued popularity and given it a steadily rising monetary value.

The furniture did not appear suddenly from nowhere, but was a direct successor to plain veneered pieces like the fall-front cabinets illustrated in Plate 14 and Fig. 85. These are, however, of a fairly large size, and few small articles other than portable tables were made before 1700. After that date, the numbers began to increase rapidly, and from surviving examples it can be guessed, allowing for a large percentage that has vanished, that they were once plentiful.

The large-sized bureau-cabinet evolved from the sloping-top escritoire or scriptor, beneath which were placed drawers and on top of which was stood a two-door cabinet. Examples vary in the treatment of door-tops and pediments, which were made flat, double-domed, or angled according to taste and the depth of the buyer's pocket. Internal fittings differed also in complexity and quality, and in many instances the hinged front enclosed a well concealed by a sliding top. This occupied the space ostensibly taken up by all or some of the topmost drawer, which in such cases was given a dummy front.

The fronts of bureaux, when open, are supported by a pair of flat arms which slide into the carcass when not required for use (see Figs. 138 and 139). In most examples a sliding candle-holder is fitted immediately below each door, making use of the mirror-glass as a reflector. The glass was invariably bevelled, and if genuine it will be found that the bevelling is very gradual and quite

different from modern sharply-angled work. The latter has a hard and clearly visible ridge along its apex, whereas 18th-Century 'diamonding' can scarcely be felt with the finger and is not always obvious to the eye. It is as well to remember, however, that not only can the blue-grey colouring of old glass be imitated, but the soft bevelling can be copied.

Both of the double-domed cabinets in Figs. 135 and 136 are veneered with burr walnut on their fronts, while straight-grained wood is used for the sides where it is less noticeable. The interior fittings in the upper part of Fig. 136 are of pronounced complexity, and comprise drawers of various shapes and sizes, pigeon-holes and a central cupboard. The Corinthian columns flanking the latter pull out to reveal hidden containers, and it is not unusual for others to be concealed elsewhere. Often some of the drawers do not run to the full depth of the cabinet, and when they are removed hidden ones are discovered. Of the many hundreds that have been found over the years, very few indeed contain anything to reward the excitement and hopes of their finders.

The four narrow single-door bureaux-cabinets in Plate 23 and Figs. 137, 138, and 139 are also veneered on their fronts with burr walnut and their sides plainly straight-grained. Two of them bear the labels of their makers: John Phillips (Fig. 138) and William Old and John Ody (Fig. 139), which gives them additional interest as it has enabled a number of unlabelled examples of comparable appearance to be attributed to the same sources.

The small circular printed label of John Phillips gives his London address as 'at the Cabinet the South Side of St. Paul's', an address at which he is recorded in 1725. The date when he commenced business there is

not known, but an announcement in 1732 stated that he

> Is removed from St. Paul's Church Yard to *The Cabinet*, against St. Peter's Church, in Cornhill, near the Royal Exchange.[1]

The Churchyard, an area surrounding St. Paul's Cathedral, was the location of a number of businesses, particularly those of booksellers and cabinet-makers. Before

Opposite, *Fig. 139: Walnut bureau-cabinet, the latticed single door flanked by pilasters and surmounted by a moulded broken pediment. With the label of William Old and John Ody 'at the Castle in St. Paul's Church-Yard'. Early 18th Century; width 76·2 cm. (Phillips, Son and Neale.)* **Below,** *Fig. 140: Walnut bureau on stand, surmounted by a walnut and gesso framed looking-glass. Early 18th Century; width 62·2 cm. (Christie's.)*

---

[1] *Ambrose Heal,* London Furniture Makers, 1660–1840, *1953, pages 137 and 254.*

the edifice was rebuilt, following its destruction in the Great Fire, the nave and other portions of the building had been similarly used, and many 16th- and 17th-Century writers deplored the inappropriate intrusion there of commerce. Lawyers interviewed their clients, discussed their cases and each 'took notes thereof upon his knee'; servants sought employment; the font served as a counter for payments; and in 1629 it was noted that 'the noyse in it is like that of Bees, in strange hummings or buzze, mixt of walking, tongues, and feet; it is a kind of still roare, or loud whisper'. All this ceased on the completion of Wren's task, when traders were confined to the outside of the building.

Fig. 141: Bureau and stand veneered and cross-banded with burr and straight-grained walnut, the cabriole legs with lions' mask knees and hairy claw-and-ball feet. Early 18th Century; width 81·3 cm. (Christie's.)

William Old and John Ody were active at about the same time as Phillips, and their premises were not far distant from each other. The trade label of the former depicts a fortified castle bristling with cannon and with pennants flying from its towers, the whole framed in a composition of Corinthian columns topped by urns, linked by an arch and standing upon leafy scrolls. The wording reads:

> WILLIAM OLD AND JOHN ODY At the Castle in St. Paul's Church-Yard, over-against the South-Gate of yᵉ Church, London, Makes and Sells all sorts of Cane & Dutch Chairs, Chair Frames for Stuffing and Cane-Sashes. And also all sorts of the best Looking-Glass & Cabinet-Work in Japan, Walnut-Tree & Wainscot, at reasonable Rates.[1]

William Old died at some date prior to 1738, in which year the stock-in-trade of 'the late widow Old' was offered for sale on the premises. John Ody became a liveryman of the Joiners' Company in 1723, and apart from these few facts there is at present no information about the two men.

Of these small cabinets it was pointed out by R. W. Symonds that their very restricted writing-space made them impractical in use, a width of two feet or so (about 60 cm.) being likely to cramp the style of even a determined correspondent. He came to the conclusion that they were made to stand 'against the pier wall between the windows of the standard type of brick house which was built in large numbers during the first half of the 18th Century, a position which would have the advantage of catching the light from both windows'. Symonds noted also that as some of them had their top drawers fitted with covered boxes and divisions and sometimes additionally a small looking-glass, it was probable that they served for dressing.

Of this variety is the piece of furniture in Fig. 140, which was at one time in the

---

[1] *Ibid., page 130.*

ownership of Percival Griffiths. The swing glass is bevelled and framed in moulded walnut with an inner border of carved and gilt gesso, the sloping front encloses the usual drawers and pigeon-holes, while the uppermost drawer in the base is fitted with boxes and divisions. The cabriole legs on which it is raised have only a slight curve to them, the knees are each carved with a formal shell and leaf motif and the feet are moulded. An unusual feature is that the drawer-linings are of mahogany, whereas normally they are oak or, in the case of the small inside drawers, of solid walnut.

The bureau illustrated in Fig. 141 is of more sophisticated design than the preceding pieces, while it is also of slightly later date than any of them. The top drawer beneath the slope is fitted with a slide, which suggests that it, too, may have served as a dressing-table. The base has hipped cabriole legs, boldly carved on the knees with lions' masks and terminating in hairy claw-and-ball feet. The frieze or apron of the base is carved with a central shell flanked by leaves, and it is notable that the back legs, which so often are left quite plain, are in this instance carved on the knees and have club feet.

The cabinet shown in Plate 24 (facing page 190) is of greater width than those just discussed, but shares with them the merit of bearing the name of its maker. In this instance it is not printed on a slip of paper stuck casually in a drawer, but is unusual in being inlaid in wood. The inside of the door is bordered with veneer to simulate two pilasters, and at the base of them runs the inscription: 'Samuel Bennett London Fecit'. Two other signed examples of the work of the same maker have been recorded, one of which is also inlaid with his name while the second has the more commonplace paper label.

The latter gives a little more information about the man, including the fact that he was not too careful about the spelling of his surname. It reads:

Samuel Bennet Cabinet-maker, at the Sign of the Cabinet in *Lothbury*, Maketh and Selleth all sorts of Fine Cabinet-Work and Looking-Glasses, at Reasonable Rates.

He is known to have been in occupation of the premises in Lothbury, which runs along the north side of the Bank of England, in 1723, and to have died in 1741.

One of the Bennett cabinets is distinctive in having a boldly curved base which is shaped on both the sides as well as the front; a shape often found on Dutch and other Continental furniture of the time but rare in England. A cabinet with a similarly *bombé*

Fig. 142: Walnut secretaire-cabinet, the upper part fitted with two glazed doors surmounted by a broken pediment centred on a gilt shell, and the bombé lower part mounted with cut brass on the front corners and raised on moulded low feet. Circa 1725; width 112 cm. (Sotheby's)

lower part is illustrated in Fig. 142. This one has the top drawer fitted with a hinged front which falls to reveal a writing surface and fittings, while the broken pediment centres on a large gilt shell. The projecting lower corners of the base are protected by brass mounts cut in a foliate pattern, again a rarity in England at this date.

Reverting to small-sized pieces, the bureau in Fig. 143 is remarkable. The narrowness of many of these semi-miniatures is their undoubted attraction, although, as mentioned, the allowance of writing-space is both inconvenient and

uncomfortable. The present example has ten drawers in the lower part, and a cupboard inset within what is little more than a vestigial kneehole.

A kneehole space is also a feature of many flat-topped tables like the one in Fig. 144, which may have served for either writing or dressing. Many past writers railed against the excessive use of cosmetics and listed at length the many requirements of a fashionable lady, which ranged from perfumes and paints to patches and artificial eyebrows cut from mouse-skin. Their small capacity may suggest that tables like these were intended for use by the less worldly, or simply for the penning of the briefest *billets-doux.*

More practical for normal usage are bureaux and secretaires permitting full freedom of movement. The tallboy-secretaire in Fig. 145 is a good example of a popular type, with burr walnut veneer bordered with herring-bone and crossbanding. The front of the base and the centre of the lowest drawer are shaped to emphasise the sunburst inlaid in ebony and holly which is a feature of the drawer, while the front corners of the whole are canted and fluted.

To the names of makers mentioned above may be added those of Hugh Granger and Giles Grendey. The former's address was The Carved Angel, Aldermanbury, where his stock was sold in 1706 on account of 'the house being let to another trade' (Fig. 146). Grendey had his premises at Aylesbury House, St. John's Square, Clerkenwell, was born in 1693 and died at the age of 87 in 1780. His label, which is a simple printed one, reads:

GILES GRENDEY, St. John's Square, Clerkenwell, LONDON, MAKES and

Sells all Sorts of CABINET GOODS, Chairs, Tables, Glasses, &c.

It has been found on both mahogany and japanned furniture, the latter including two large suites of chairs (see Plate 17) with a settee and a day bed, which had been in private ownership in Spain since they were supplied. That he did business with foreign clients is borne out by newspaper reports of a fire at Aylesbury House in 1731, when it was reported that furniture to the value of a thousand pounds, 'pack'd for Exportation against the Morning', had been lost.

English labelled furniture of any date is scarce, and that of the first half of the 18th Century is especially so. The number of makers who troubled to record their names and addresses in this manner is undiscovered and will probably remain unknown. It is uncertain what proportion of their total output each may have marked, and whether they conferred this distinction only on goods for special customers or for export. It is remarkable that none of the Royal cabinetmakers labelled their work, although Moore and Gumley did carve their names occasionally.

It is impossible to know how many labels have been removed and lost in the course of time. They are small and very vulnerable; easily removed by those of a destructive nature who were irritated by them and ignorant of their historical value. Many must still remain unnoticed in pieces of furniture that are in daily use. In the majority of instances the label was stuck in the centre of the bottom of a drawer, where it might be seen by anyone pulling it open. On chairs, of which only one of a set was usually labelled, a label would be found on the framing beneath the seat.

Left, *Fig. 146: Walnut bureau-cabinet, the door inset with looking-glass concealing the interior decorated with Chinese scenes in gold on a red ground, and the whole raised on square cabriole legs. With the label of Hugh Granger 'at The Carved Angell in Aldermanbury'. Early 18th Century; width 56·5 cm. (Christie's.)*

Right, *Plate 24: Bureau-cabinet of walnut inlaid with other woods, by Samuel Bennett. Inside the door is the inlaid inscription:* Samuel Bennett London fecit. *Circa 1720; width 95·8 cm. (Victoria and Albert Museum.)*

13: 'Queen Anne Walnut' — Chairs, Chests, Tables

THE appearance of chairs, as much as that of any other pieces of furniture, benefited from the use of walnut. Although the timber lacked the great strength of oak, its close grain and comparative softness per-

Left, *Fig. 147: Chair of walnut inlaid with holly in patterns of strapwork, scrolls and other motifs. Circa 1710.* **Below,** *Fig. 148: Walnut chair with cabriole legs and turned under-stretchers. Circa 1710. (Bearnes & Waycotts.)*

mitted much greater freedom to the carver. The Restoration saw, among so many other stylistic changes, the chair-back grow elongated until its height from the ground became about three times that of the seat.

To prevent the article toppling over, the rear legs were made to slope backwards, while to brace the lower part of the frame one or more stretchers linked all four legs. It is probable, however, that the more elaborate examples were meant for display; standing before the walls of great apartments to complete a scheme of decoration, they were not intended for use. This would have been the case with the chairs having open-worked wood or wood and caned backs, as well as those covered in expensive fringed silks.

Some of the latter variety are seen in Daniel Marot's designs reproduced in Fig. 87 (page 110), while a specimen exhibiting some of the features popularised by Marot and his contemporaries is in Fig. 149. The very tall back rises to a pierced and carved scroll and leaf cresting, the centre of the back is filled with a shaped splat of matching pattern, while the cabriole front legs with carved knees have scroll toes above shaped pads. The back legs are plain, and united to those in front by scrolled side-stretchers which, in turn, are joined by a further stretcher, carved and placed almost centrally.

The general complexity of the design, the serpentine shaping of the front rail and the

high standard of execution suggest that this chair was made in the Netherlands. Nonetheless, it may be argued that a Dutch cabinet-maker domiciled in London could equally have been responsible for it. Proof will probably never be forthcoming, but despite doubt as to which side of the Channel saw its origin it is agreed that it was made in about 1700.

Within a decade a less formal-looking chair had evolved; the back less tall and the whole with a more inviting appearance to those seeking rest. The cabriole leg became the most common support, and terminated according to taste in a round 'pad' foot, a moulded angled one or a cloven hoof. The leg itself was a revival of the conventionalised animals' legs used in Greek and Roman furniture. The term is derived from the French and Italian, the word *capriola* in the latter tongue meaning a goat's leap, but has been applied to the chair leg only in comparatively modern times and a contemporary name for it appears to be unrecorded.

The plain cabriole leg is shown in Figs. 147 and 148. The former chair is neatly inlaid in light-coloured wood with patterns of strapwork, scrolls and other motifs, while the second chair has a plain but more elaborate splat and the legs are joined by stretchers. In both examples the seats are of the drop-in variety, which are easily removable for re-covering. The multiplicity of elegant curves embodied in the design of both chairs is proof of their makers' technical skill, while the fact that they have remained in sound condition for two and a half centuries is a tribute to the shrewd selection of the timber and the care they have received from successive owners.

The chair in Fig. 150 is somewhat later in date and more advanced in design than the preceding two. The back, including the splat, and the framing of the seat are veneered with burr walnut, the legs being cut from the solid wood. It relies on the figuring of the grain and the general shaping of the whole for its decorative effect,

Above, *Fig. 149: Walnut tall-back chair with carved and pierced decoration. Circa 1700. (Christie's.)*

Left, *Plate 25: Veneered walnut 'Bachelor's Chest' fitted with drawers and a folding top. Circa 1720; width 85 cm. (Stourhead, Wiltshire: The National Trust.)*

with only a minimum of carving in the form of scallop shells on the apron and knees. The front feet each terminate in a claw grasping a ball; a foot employed in England in Tudor times and which, after making a brief re-appearance during the reign of Charles II, was again popular between about 1725 and 1760.

By the turn of the 17th Century the craft of chair-making had become separate from other branches of furniture manufacture, and the names of some of the men who may have specialised in it have been noted.

Above, *Fig. 150: Chair veneered with walnut, the cabriole legs with carved knees and claw-and-ball feet.* Circa *1720. (Christie's.)*

Right, *Fig. 151: Walnut 'Library Arm-chair' on cabriole legs with pad feet. Circa 1715. (Royal Ontario Museum, Toronto, Canada: photograph, John Keil Ltd.)*

Amongst them were Thomas Roberts, who worked for both William III and Queen Anne, and a relative of his, Richard Roberts, who supplied George I and was described as 'Chairmaker to His Majesty'.

Although it was written a few decades after the period under discussion, an account published in 1747 is applicable to the early part of the century. It appeared in *A General Description of All Trades* '. . . by which Parents, Guardians, and Trustees, may, with greater Ease and Certainty, make choice of Trades agreeable to the Capacity, Education, Inclination, Strength, and For-

tune of the Youth under their Care', and gave the following paragraphs under the heading of 'Chair-Makers':

Though this Sort of Houshold Goods is generally sold at the Shops of the *Cabinet-makers* for all the better Kinds, and at the *Turners* for the more common, yet there are particular Makers for each.

The *Cane-chair-makers* not only make this Sort, (now almost out of Use) but the better Sort of matted, Leather-bottomed, and Wooden Chairs, of all which there is great Variety in Goodness, Workmanship, and Price; and some of the Makers, who are also Shop-keepers, are very considerable Dealers, employing from 300 to upwards of 500 *l.* in Trade, and require with an Apprentice 10 *l.* The Work is pretty smart, the Hours from six to nine; and a Journeyman's Wages 12 *s.* a Week.

The white Wooden, Wicker, and ordinary matted Sort, commonly called Kitchen-chairs, and sold by the *Turners* are made by different Hands, but are all inferior Employs. Those covered with Stuffs, Silks, *&c.* are made and sold by the *Upholsterers*.

Chairs were made in sets ranging in number up to a dozen and more, and sometimes including armchairs to match. A number of the latter are recorded that would probably never have been ensuite with singles, but were made to a special pattern and for a particular purpose. In this category are the chairs presumably for use at a writing-desk, of which the arms are designed to cause a minimum of inconvenience to the user. An example is illustrated in Fig. 151, and others of comparable pattern are known both in single specimens and pairs. In these last instances, as it would seem that no more than one would be required for a desk, it may be thought that an appropriate accurate description for them would be 'Library Armchairs' which covers both writing and reading.

From the Restoration onwards, stools were made closer to the ground, and the

tall, long-enduring and serviceable joint-stool was replaced by a more decorative article. Their formal use on important occasions[1] continued into the 18th Century, and as late as 1735 the etiquette of *tabouret*, imported with its name from France, was current at the Court of George II. On the eve of the marriage of Frederick Louis, Prince of Wales, to Princess Augusta of Saxe-Gotha, the bride was entertained to mid-day dinner at St. James's Palace by her bridegroom. The guests were his brother and sisters, and before the meal began an angry scene took place when the latter refused to sit on stools while Augusta and Frederick occupied chairs. The stools were eventually exchanged for chairs, the argument being that Augusta was not entitled to a chair until her marriage and the others felt insulted at being offered inferior seats.[2]

Late 17th-Century stools showed many of the features of chairs of the time, with scrolled legs and similar cross-stretchers.

While many were rectangular in shape, others were circular-topped. The cabriole leg was employed with good effect, as in the example in Fig. 152 (right), which is of walnut ornamented with carved and gilt gesso. Such treatment was rare, and examples of this mixture of wood and gilding are termed 'parcel-gilt'; a revival of the old term 'parcel', meaning partly. The other stool illustrated below (left) is of a more conventional type, with finely-shaped cabriole legs and claw-and-ball feet.

The foregoing stools, like many chairs from the late 17th Century onwards, have covers of petit-point needlework. The fashion for this, like the mania for collecting china, was due to Queen Mary. Gilbert

---

[1] *See pages 8 and 94.*

[2] *Averyl Edwards, op. cit., page 58.*

Burnet, Bishop of Salisbury from 1689, wrote of her:

> . . . in all hours that were not given to better employment she wrought with her own hands, and sometimes with so constant a diligence as if she had been to earn her bread by it. It was a new thing, and looked a sight, to see a Queen work so many hours a day.

The Royal workmanship was commented on by Celia Fiennes when she paid a visit to Hampton Court in the early 1700's, and noted:

> Out of the dressing roome is the Queens Closet, the hangings, Chaires, Stooles and Screen the same, all of satten stitch done in worsteds, beasts, birds, images, and ffruites all wrought very finely by Queen Mary and her maids of honour.[1]

More than a century earlier another Mary, Mary Queen of Scots, had shown a liking for similar work, although it was performed under very different circumstances. While imprisoned in Lochleven Castle in 1567 she requested that she might have five servants, of whom one should be 'an imbroderer to drawe forth such worke as she would be occupied about'. During her long imprisonment in England, between 1558 and her execution in 1587, she spent much of her time embroidering panels, of which some have been preserved and may be seen in the Victoria and Albert Museum and elsewhere.[2]

Although the backs and seats of chairs and the seats of stools were suitable for needlework covers, the larger surfaces of settees and wing-armchairs were even more effective. This is exemplified in the armchair in Fig. 153; which was designed not only to keep the occupant free from draughts but was fitted with a ratchet mechanism, so that

---

[1] *Op. cit., page 305.*

[2] *Margaret H. Swain, op. cit., pages 13–21.*

the back might be adjusted to provide the maximum personal comfort. The needle-work is in a pattern of oversize flowers and foliage on a blue ground, and the seat cushion is removable.

The walnut chest of drawers differed in various respects in Queen Anne's day from its forerunners in the 1680's. Figured walnut veneers with cross-banded borders and intervening herring-bone inlays were in general use, and many examples were of smaller size than hitherto. The most

Below, *Fig. 154: 'Bachelor's Chest' made of 'wanscoate' (wainscot) oak. Circa 1725; width about 76 cm. (Mallett & Son Ltd.)*

Right, *Fig. 155: Walnut chest of drawers with folding top (Bachelor's Chest). Circa 1725; width about 76 cm. (Mallett & Son Ltd.)*

notable constructional advance is to be seen in the finish of drawer-fronts, which were usually framed by a narrow projecting rounded moulding known as a 'cock-bead' (Fig. 155 and Plate 23). Further, while the front of the drawer had been dovetailed to the sides from soon after the mid-17th Century, a half-century or so later it became usual to dovetail the back also. An alternative to the cock bead was provided by a curved moulding overlapping the drawer-front, which covered the opening in the

Left, *Fig. 156: 'Bachelor's Chest' veneered with laburnum, the folding top concealing a rising till released by the knob on the left. (John Keil Ltd.)*

Below, *Fig. 157: The same with the top raised. Circa 1725; width 79 cm.*

carcass and not only kept dust from entering but resulted in a neat finish (Figs. 154 and 156).

In modern times the most popular of the numerous surviving walnut chests are the small specimens with a fold-over top, the latter hinged at the front corners unlike the card-table which is hinged at the back. Lopers support the opened top, and slide away at each side of the top drawer when they are not required. The chests are known nowadays as 'Bachelor's Chests', but when or why they acquired the name is unknown. Perhaps it originated in the

same ingenious mind that gave the name 'Bachelor Teapot' to a small-capacity teapot; a name which also has an indeterminate origin.

While the chest in Fig. 155 is veneered with walnut, that in Fig. 154 is solid oak. While it would have been more common to

find such articles in the homes of average citizens, its use was not confined to any one level of society and 'wanscoate' was to be found in palaces as well as cottages. The third of these small-sized chests, of which two views are shown (Figs. 156 and 157), is unusual because it is fitted with a rising till. This is released by the small knob seen to the left, and the till remains in place by means of the flat springy boards at each side of it. In addition, it is veneered with laburnum, which has a distinctive contrasting striped marking.

Some further types of tables remain to be discussed. That in Fig. 158 was probably intended for use as a writing-table, although it would serve equally well for dressing.

Left, *Fig. 158: Three-drawer writing or dressing table veneered with walnut, the legs and stretchers of solid wood.* Circa *1690; width 77·5 cm.* (Mallett & Son Ltd.)

Below, *Fig. 159: Card table veneered with walnut, the inner two back legs hinged to support the top.* Circa *1700; width 84 cm.* (Mallett & Son Ltd.)

The drawer-openings are framed by mouldings and the shaped apron rises in the centre to form a small kneehole. Later versions of the same three-drawer type have cabriole legs with claw-and-ball feet, while the drawers are cock-beaded.

Common to most houses from early times were card-tables, and walnut examples are among the more pleasing of them. The one in Fig. 159 has six supports, of which two at the back swing outwards to support the top when it is opened flat. The faceted legs are linked by a flat shaped stretcher and the feet are turned. The later cabriole legs on the table in Fig. 160 terminate in claw-and-ball feet, while the inside of the top has recesses at each corner for holding money or counters. The table bears the label of Benjamin Crook, and is inscribed within a circle of scrollwork:

> All Sorts of Cabinet Work Mahogony Tables Looking Glasses Chairs &c. Made & Sold by Benj. Crook at yᵉ George & White Lyon on yᵉ South Side of St. Pauls Church Yard LONDON.

During one of her numerous 'Journeys' Celia Fiennes visited Windsor. This was in about 1703, and she has left a clear, if rather breathless word-picture of the interior of a Royal residence which is probably applicable to numerous other houses of the day. Paintings depicting such settings were not then fashionable, but she has fortunately left for us on paper what is missing on canvas. The under-mentioned is an extract of what she saw, and her words provide a fitting close to 'Queen Anne Walnut':

> On the Right hand is a Large Antyroome for persons to wait, where are Marble tables in yᵉ Peeres between the windows; white damaske window curtaines and cane chaires. Next it is the Dineing roome some stepps down, where was red silk Curtaines Chaires and stooles, and Benches round the roome all red silk, wᵗʰ some coull'd orrice Lace[1]; here was a white marble table behind the doore as a sideboard, and a Clap table[2] under yᵉ Large

Looking Glass between the windows. Next this was a drawing roome; both these roomes were hung wᵗʰ small Jmage tapistry very Lively and ffresh, here was Crimson Damaske window Curtaines, Chaires and stooles. The next was what was Prince George's[3] dressing roome, hung, and window Curtaines Chaires and stooles, all wᵗʰ yellow damaske, wᵗʰ marble Chimney pieces as all yᵉ Roomes have of Differing Coullrs black white, grey, rance[4] &c &c. Large Looking-glasses; all the roomes in all yᵉ house is plaine unvarnished oake Wanscoate which Lookes very neate. Wᵗʰin the dressing

---

[1] *Orrice lace contained gold and silver thread.*

[2] *A Clap table was one which could be folded and put aside when not in use.*

[3] *Prince George of Denmark was married to Princess (later Queen) Anne in 1683. He died in 1708.*

[4] *Rance was a red marble with blue and white markings.*

roome is a Closet on one hand, the other side is a Closet y^t Leads to a little place wth a seate of Easement of Marble wth sluces of water to wash all down. There is a back doore in y^e dressing roome, to a little anty roome with presses, a little Wanscoate table for tea, cards or writeing, so to a back staires . . . .[1]

[1] *Op. cit., pages 306–7.*

Above, Fig. 160: Walnut veneered card table, the drawer in the frieze with the label of the maker, Benjamin Crook of St. Paul's Churchyard, London. Circa 1730; width 85 cm. (Christie's.)

14 : Tables and Frames

THE burst of scientific interest that coincided with the Restoration led not only to improvements in mechanical devices, but to an enhanced appreciation of natural phenomena. The published papers of the Royal Society show how widespread was the activity, with the result that human knowledge increased at a hitherto unprecedented rate.

The study of natural history as a means to improving the lot of mankind led to the formation of collections of numerous different objects, among which were stones of many kinds. Recording what he saw when he was in Paris in 1698, Dr Martin Lister, a member of the Royal Society, noted:

> I visited Monsieur Morin, one of the Academie des Sciences, a Man very curious in Minerals; of which he showed me some from Siam, as Jaspers, Onyxes, Agats, Loadstones, &c.

It was by no means a fresh pursuit, for Tudor travellers returning from journeys into Europe and farther afield had brought back with them comparable trophies. In particular, visitors to Florence reported with enthusiasm on the skilful local craftmanship flourishing there under the patronage of the Medicis. When he founded it in about 1580 the Grand Duke Francesco I had intended the *Opificio delle Pietre Dure*

to serve as a source of supply for his court. From its output he would be able to furnish his palaces and make gifts to dazzle visitors from near and far.

The *Opificio* was duly installed in the Uffizi and remained there until it was removed to the Via degli Alfani in 1796, where a museum was later set up and became one of the sights of the city. Among the many who reported seeing examples of the work was John Evelyn, who was in Florence in October 1644 and wrote in his diary:

> Under the Court of Justice is a stately arcade for men to walke in, and over that, the shops of divers rare artists who continually worke for the greate Duke. Above this is the renowned Ceimeliarcha, or Repository, wherein are hundreds of admirable antiquities, statues of marble and mettal, vasas of porphyrie, &c. ... Here were divers tables of Pietro Comessa, which is a marble ground inlay'd with severall sorts of marbles and stones of various colours, representing flowers, trees, beasts, birds, and landskips. In one is represented the towne of Ligorne by the same hand who inlay'd the altar of St. Lawrence, Domenico Benotti, of whom I purchased 19 pieces of the same worke for a cabinet.

The panels were brought safely to England

Left, *Plate 27: Cabinet inset with panels of Italian* pietre dure *and mounted on a stand decorated with gilt gesso.* Circa *1730; width about 107 cm.* (Mallett & Son Ltd.)

Above, *Fig. 161: Panel of* pietre dure, *similar to those in the cabinet in Plate 27. Italian, early 18th Century.* (Private collection.)

and duly mounted in a cabinet which remains in the possession of Evelyn's descendants.

Others returning from a Grand Tour purchased similar trophies, and likewise had them mounted. An example is illustrated in Plate 27, where the inlaid marble landscapes form a colourful contrast to the black woodwork in which they are set. The columns and plinths of marble and the gilt ornamentation of the stand, cresting and mouldings give the piece additional decorative value. It may be compared with a well-known cabinet made at a later date for Elizabeth, Duchess of Manchester, once at Kimbolton Castle and now in the Victoria and Albert Museum. Designed in 1771 by Robert Adam to display some plaques signed and dated 1709, it was made by the London cabinet-makers Ince and Mayhew with the aid of gilt-bronze mounts supplied by Matthew Boulton.[1] Altogether it is remarkably well documented in contrast to the lack of such information about most other examples.

Inlaid marble in the manner of the Italian *pietre dure* was executed in England but began at a much later date. Writing in about 1840, William Adam, proprietor of Mawe's Old Museum at Matlock, Derbyshire, stated:

> . . . the beautiful style so long adopted at Florence, was introduced into Matlock ten years ago by the author, the first specimen being a butterfly. . . .

---

[1] *Lindsay Boynton, 'An Ince and Mayhew Correspondence', in* Furniture History *II (1966), page 23.*

This work advanced from butterflies to sprigs, birds, flowers, and foliage of every description, and some of the most beautiful designs and perfect workmanship are now done in this country, and introduced as ornamental tables, inlaid vases, &c., into many of the first noblemen's houses. Many of the beautiful scrolls and borders on the Shah Jehan's tomb at Agra, [the Taj Mahal] have been exactly copied.[1]

William Adam wrote further that there was at Windsor Castle 'a magnificent table, inlaid with a wreath of flowers and foliage, with birds, butterflies, &c., placed most judiciously on different parts of the wreath, which completely encircled a large slab of fine black marble, and was elegantly mounted on a stand of the same material'.

He added that Queen Victoria had purchased it from his establishment in 1842.

The description of the table and its decoration makes it clear that although the technique employed in Derbyshire was the same as the earlier Florentine, the results were completely different. There should be no difficulty in distinguishing between them, for Victorian taste in subject-matter and the colours chosen for their portrayal cannot be confused with those of any other period.

The liking for colourful and preferably rare stones was not confined to small-sized specimens, and large slabs were eagerly sought. In view of the immense difficulties caused by primitive roads and lack of mechanical power, heavy loads were sent as far as possible by sea and overland journeys cut to a minimum. From the first decades

[1] *W. Adam*, The Gem of the Peak, *4th edition, 1845, page 408.*

Above, *Fig. 163; Walnut side table, the frieze carved with a lion's mask and skin. The cabriole legs have hairy claw-and-ball feet, and the top is of green marble. Circa 1735; width 104 cm. (Christie's.)*

of the 18th Century a continual supply of marble left Italy, in particular, but also other countries with suitable attractive material, to grace the homes of Englishmen.

Not all was imported, and Daniel Defoe noted in the 1720's in Dorsetshire, that

> There are also several Rocks of very good Marble, only that the Veins in the Stone are not Black and White, as the *Italian*, but Grey, Red, and other Colours.[1]

Farther north, at Bakewell, Derbyshire, Anthony Berrisford proclaimed his willingness to supply 'English & Foreign Marbles' in all shapes, 'Done in the Best manner, And at Reasonable Rates'. No doubt he was not alone in performing this service, but fortunately his trade card has been preserved while traces of the existence of most of his fellow-craftsmen have vanished.

---

[1] Tour Through Great Britain, *1727, re-published in 2 vols. 1927, vol. I, page 209.*

ENGLISH marbles had their admirers, but foreign specimens commanded more general admiration. It was due not only to the glamour attached to anything brought with difficulty from a distance, but to their more interesting and colourful appearance. It was possible to meet the demand for examples with the desired characteristics by staining and marking the sober-looking English varieties, and this was done occasionally from the late 17th Century onwards. John Dossie, who compiled a two-volume manual of useful receipts entitled *The Handmaid of the Arts*, published in 1758 and reissued slightly altered in 1764, devoted two paragraphs to the subject. He headed them 'Of staining alabaster, marble

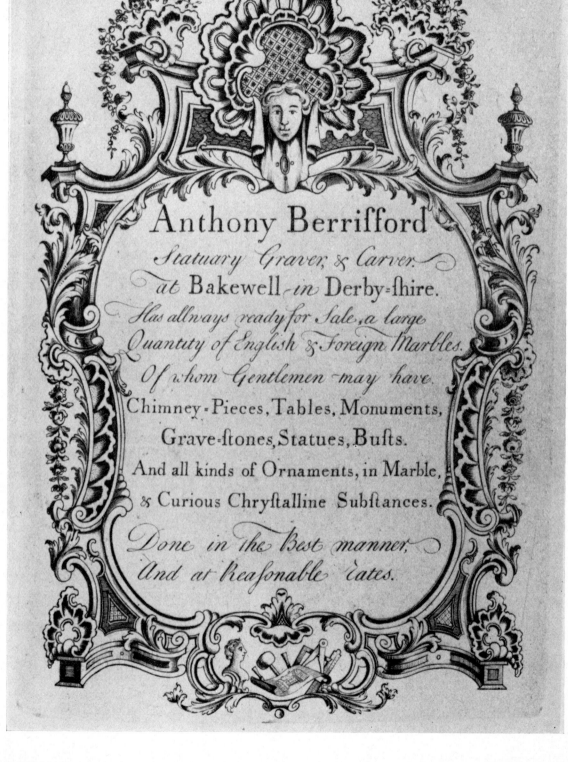

Anthony Berrisford
Statuary Graver, & Carver.
at Bakewell in Derby=shire.
Has allways ready for Sale, a large
Quantity of English & Foreign Marbles.
Of whom Gentlemen may have.
Chimney=Pieces, Tables, Monuments,
Grave=stones, Statues, Busts.
And all kinds of Ornaments, in Marble,
& Curious Chrystalline Substances.

Done in the Best manner,
And at Reasonable 'eates.

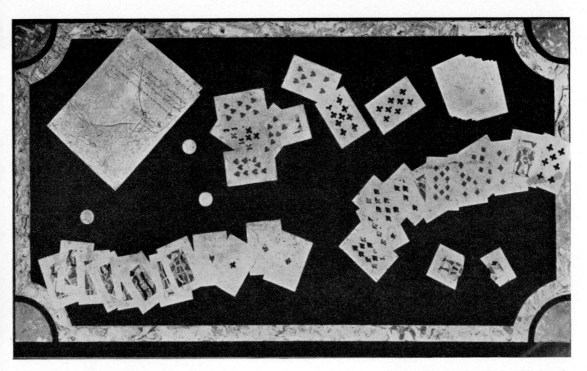

Left, *Fig. 164: The tradesman's card of Anthony Berrisford of Bakewell, Derbyshire. He was a supplier of English and foreign marbles in the mid-18th Century, and his card is one of the few surviving today.*

Above, *Fig. 165: Scagliola table top, the letter at the top left referring to the Treaty of Utrecht and dated 20th May 1713. Circa 1715; width 106·7 cm. (Saltram, Devon; The National Trust.)*

and other stones, of various colours', and suggests the use of stains employed normally for wood, which should be brushed or poured on the work. It was not a very ambitious method, as there was no attempt to simulate the much-admired markings distinguishing the best varieties from the commonplace. This had been proposed from time to time, but there are no records of whether it had been put into practice with or without success.

Stain was, however, employed with great effect in Italy, where a 'school' of craftsmen working in and around Florence imitated *pietre dure* with a material named *scagliola*. The basis of the composition was pulverised selenite, a variety of gypsum quarried in the locality, which could be made into an inexpensive substitute for all kinds of marble. It could be coloured as required,

when hard took a high polish, and when inlaid in real marble formed an acceptable substitute for, if not an improvement on, the expensive products of the Grand Duke's workshops.

Don Enrico Hugford, Abbot of the Monastery of S. Reparata at Marradi, was given training in the *scagliola* technique by the monks there. Born in 1695, he was the earliest craftsman to achieve fame at the work, although very little of his output has been identified. To him is due the credit for raising *scagliola* from being merely a cheap imitation of inlaid marble to an individual form of applied art.

An early 18th-Century *scagliola* table-top is shown above, and can be dated to about 1715. The marble is inlaid with a realistically-coloured representation of some playing-cards, three counters and a letter. The last is dated London, 20 May 1713, is signed 'John Pollexfen', and contains the information that 'this day yᵉ peace between Englᵈ and France was proclaimᵈ here by yᵉ heralds as is usual in such cases'. The reference is to the Treaty of Utrecht, signed on 11 April 1713, which terminated the War of the Spanish Succession.

While Enrico Hugford's predecessors remain in obscurity, one of his pupils took the trouble to sign his handiwork and details about it have been recorded.[1] Personal details about the man himself, Don Petro Belloni, are lacking except for the fact that dated examples of his work show that he was active at least between about 1745 and 1755. Horace Walpole corresponded with his friend Sir Horace Mann, the British envoy at Florence, about obtaining for a friend two of Belloni's table-tops.

They were ordered in 1747 and only finished three years later, while two others made for an Irish buyer took as long as six years before they were finally ready for shipment. Whether the delays were due to Don Petro's temperament or to the nature of the work is not known.

---

[1] *See Anthony Coleridge, 'Don Petro's Table-tops', in* Apollo, March 1966, page 184.

Below, *Fig. 166: Design for a side table, by Matthias Lock. Circa 1740. Pencil drawing; width 17·5 cm. (Victoria & Albert Museum.)*

When Celia Fiennes wrote of seeing in the Dining Room at Hampton Court 'a white marble table behind the doore as a side-board', she referred not to the entire table but only to the top. It was the latter which was then and for the rest of the century the most important feature, and whatever supported the slab was dismissed by her as not being worth reporting. A few all-marble tables and tops were made from time to time, but they were few in number and in most instances a reference by Celia Fiennes or anyone else to 'a Table' means what we term nowadays a table-top. The support was called a 'Frame', and appears as such in bills and other records which have been preserved: Thomas Chippendale printed designs for them under the title 'Frames for Marble Slabs'.

Many of the frames made in the early decades of the 18th Century were of large size, and their design, like that of the houses for which they were made, was sometimes the work of professional architects. The name of William Kent is prominent among them (see Fig. 119, page 154), but Henry Flitcroft and John Vardy have also been held responsible for examples. Flitcroft, like Kent, was a protégé of the Earl of Burlington, whose patronage he gained through 'the accident of falling from a scaffold and breaking a leg while working

Below, Fig 167: Gilt wood side table. resembling the design in Fig. 166. The frieze bears a mask of Hercules draped with the skin of the Nemean lion. Circa 1740; width about 180 cm. (Bearnes & Waycotts.)

Below, *Fig. 168: Table of carved and gilt wood, the top of gesso with a design centred on the coat of arms of the Hoare family. Attributed to Henry Flitcroft (1697–1769). Circa 1730; width 121·5 cm. (Stourhead, Wiltshire: The National Trust.)* **Right,** *Fig. 169: One of a pair of pier tables, each with a seated fox biting a swag of oak leaves as a central feature and with a top of red marble. Circa 1730; width 91 cm. (Stourhead, Wiltshire: The National Trust.)*

at Burlington House'.[1] At that time he was a journeyman carpenter, but following encouragement from Lord Burlington he acquired proficiency as an architect.

A table with a *scagliola* top, the design centred on the coat of arms of the Earl of Litchfield, was once at Ditchley, Oxfordshire, and is now in the Victoria and Albert Museum. Because Flitcroft worked in the

[1] *H. M. Colvin, op. cit., page 206.*

Below, Fig. 170: Painted and gilded centre table, the legs headed with lions' masks and the wood top inlaid with a panel of marquetry on a ground of coromandel-wood crossbanded with burr yew and olive-wood. Circa 1745; width 145 cm. (Christie's.)

Below, *Fig. 171: Mahogany side table, the frieze centred on pierced scrolling leaves flanked by eagles' heads. The legs are headed with eagles' masks, and terminate in claw-and-ball feet. The top is of veined black marble.* Circa 1740; *width 160 cm.* (Saltram, Devon: The National Trust.)

house for the Earl between 1736 and 1740 it has for long been assumed that he designed the gilt frame, but there is no proper evidence that he was concerned with it. Equally unsupported is the attribution to Flitcroft of the table illustrated in Fig. 168. The top in this instance is of gilt gesso and is an unusual example of its use on a comparatively large scale, as most table-tops in the medium measure no more than a metre in width. The design includes the arms of the Hoare family, who built Stour-

head, Wiltshire, in the 18th Century. When he was creating the magnificent gardens, Henry Hoare the Younger, who inherited the estate in 1741, consulted Flitcroft about the various buildings with which the grounds became dotted, but there is no reason to suppose that the architect had any connexion with the mansion itself or with its contents.

John Vardy, another associate of Kent and his circle, is known with certainty to have designed furniture and a few of his original drawings are recorded.[1] A suite of a table and looking-glass, of which the design is in the Library of the Royal Institute of British Architects, is known,[2] and others may remain unrecognised.

An example of a table and the design for it are shown in Figs. 166 and 167. The drawing was made by Matthias Lock and was once in the ownership of his nephew, who sold it in 1862, together with many others, to the Victoria and Albert Museum. The table is not unique, as at least one other is known. The latter example varies slightly in pattern from that illustrated here, and it was once at Ditchley.[3] Had its designer's name not been known it would no doubt have been attributed to Henry Flitcroft.

On the whole, despite the appearance on them of features which occur in architecture and on other furnishings, the designers of most of the tables remain anonymous. Likewise, their makers are mostly unidentified, although with regard to the last-mentioned example it is tempting to suggest that because he was a skilful carver Lock executed it. It can be no more than a suggestion, as no proof of its authorship, or that of its near-companion, has come to light.

At Hampton Court, at the turn of the century, a 'marble table' might serve as a sideboard, but wherever they were employed they were usually more decorative than

functional. Pairs of them were placed against the piers between windows, where looking-glasses of matching design filled the wall-spaces above. Narrow examples often took the form of a well-carved eagle supporting the top on its outspread wings, and a variant of this is seen in the unusual seated fox in Fig. 169. It is one of a pair in which each animal faces forward, while on the other hand many of the eagle tables were made, also in twos, with the birds turned to regard one another.

The marble tops varied in finish according to the fashion of the time when they were made, and were given square or moulded edges accordingly. The earlier ones were solid, but later the rarer stones were cut thinly and applied to a core in the same manner as wood veneers. Derbyshire Spar ('Blue John') and lapis lazuli, for instance, were much too scarce and costly as well as

[1] *P. Ward-Jackson*, English Furniture Designs of the Eighteenth Century, *1958, pages 36–7 and figs. 39–45.*

[2] *Anthony Coleridge (John Vardy and the Hackwood Suite) in* The Connoisseur, *January 1962, page 12.*

[3] *The trusses on the front supports are inverted on the Ditchley table, which is now at Temple Newsam House, Leeds. It is illustrated in Edwards and Jourdain, op. cit., plate 82.*

Above, *Fig. 172: Mahogany side table, the cabriole legs carved on the knees with acanthus leaves and terminating in claw-and-ball feet. The top of yellow scagliola. Circa 1740; width 160 cm. (Christie's.)*

too brittle, to use in any other manner.

In Kent's day the frames were made of pine finished with gilding or paint, and carved boldly with leaves, male and female masks, sphinxes and other motifs. By about 1735 styles began to show changes, solid walnut or mahogany was employed to an increasing extent and a fresh range of details came into use. Lions' masks and eagles' heads together with the hairy claw-and-ball foot were pressed into use at every opportunity, although with innumerable variations in effect. With some of the ungilded examples personal taste played a part in substituting a top of wood in place of a marble slab. Usually they were given a border and edge of cross-banding, and sometimes an inlaid pattern as in Fig. 170.

15: The Advent of Mahogany

ALL who have paid even slight attention to 18th-Century English furniture will be familiar with the appearance of the wood from which so much of it is made: mahogany. It is a strong, reddish-brown timber, with characteristics that brought forth all the skill of the cabinet-maker and the carver, and earned enduring fame for their products.

Coming from the West Indies, it was sometimes referred to at first as 'Jamaica Wood', and R. W. Symonds noted that as early as 1661 an entry under this name appeared in the Royal accounts. In that year Thomas Malin, cabinet-maker to Charles II, supplied:

> *For Hampton Court.* For two Tables & five paire of Stands of Jamaica Wood, £18:00:00.[1]

A few years later John Ogilby listed in his book *America* 'Mohogoney' and noted its export from Jamaica. It has not been proved whether Thomas Malin used mahogany or some other wood from the same source, but certainly by about 1720 it was being brought into England in noticeable quantity. Customs records of the time present clear evidence of increasing landings, and in 1724 John Gumley and James Moore supplied for Royal use 'a mahogany supping table and two mahogany desart tables'.

A story of its first employment in London was printed in *A Book of English Trades*, published in 1821:

> The first use to which mahogany was applied in England, was to make a box for holding candles. Dr. Gibbons, an eminent physician, at the latter end of the seventeenth century, had a brother, a West-India captain, who brought over some planks of this wood as ballast. As the Doctor was then building a house in King-Street, Covent Garden, his brother thought they might be of service to him; but the carpenters finding the wood too hard for their tools, they were laid aside as useless. Soon after, Mrs. Gibbons wanting a candle-box, the Doctor called on his Cabinet-maker (Wollaston, of Long Acre) to make him one of some wood that lay in the garden. The candle-box was made, and approved; and the Doctor then insisted on having a bureau made of the same wood, which was accordingly

---

[1] *R. W. Symonds*, Furniture-making in 17th and 18th Century England, *1955, page 116.*

done; and the fine colour, polish, &c., were so pleasing, that his friends were invited to come and see it. Amongst whom was the Duchess of Buckingham. Her Grace begged some of the wood of Dr. Gibbons, and Wollaston made her a bureau also; on which the fame of the mahogany, and Mr. Wollaston, was raised, and things of this kind became general.

No dates are given by the writer, but Dr. William Gibbons lived from 1649 to 1728, and the cabinet-maker named Wollaston is known to have occupied premises in Long Acre at least between 1710 and 1720. The Duchess of Buckingham would have been Mary Fairfax, wife of the notorious second Duke, described by John Dryden as 'chemist, fiddler, statesman and buffoon'. The Duchess outlived her husband by seventeen years, dying in 1704, so the event must have taken place before then.

The mahogany imported into England in the reign of George I was the San Domingo

or Spanish, a plain straight-grained timber, appreciated not least because it was available in planks of greater width than were obtainable from any European trees. By the middle of the century attention turned to wood from Cuba, which was found to be even stronger than the other. Additionally, it showed a variety of attractive markings which allowed its optional use in the form of veneer. Time has shown another difference, because the Cuban wood retains most of its distinctive colouring, whereas the Spanish generally darkens with age until it becomes sometimes almost black.

Later, there came mahogany from the mainland forests of Honduras. It is less heavy in weight than the others, and writing in 1803 Thomas Sheraton stated that it was then 'the principal kind of mahogany in use among cabinet-makers'. It fades when exposed to strong light for any length of time, and the pale surfaces of pieces made from it in the past are esteemed nowadays to such a degree that it is not unknown for 20th-Century restorers to simulate the effect with the use of chemical bleaches.

Pre-1750 examples of carved mahogany furniture usually show the wood at its best. Good pieces of the seasoned timber were still quite expensive, and the craftsman made the best possible use of what was at his disposal. The neatness of much of the work is still remarkable after more than 200 years, and the carving retains its crispness. The quality of finish of the best carved mahogany has been compared, not unreasonably, with that of bronze, and this is exemplified in the detail shown in Fig. 174.

The foregoing depicts part of a leg of the card table reproduced in Plate 29, from which it will be seen that Spanish mahogany does not invariably retain its rich colour over the years. The table has stood for many decades with one side facing a window, so that it is now partly a nut-brown shade. A further detail photograph (Fig. 173) gives a view of the table partly closed, so that the so-called 'concertina' action is visible. This is a more expensive but more satisfactory method of constructing the supports of a folding table. When open, each leg is at a corner and the frame hinges to steady the top all along its edges. When fully extended, a board with a cut-out hand grip slides from beneath the fixed half of the top to run along a groove and keep the framework absolutely rigid.

The table is carved with a running frieze of vines centred on a shell at the back and a mask of Bacchus at the front, while the knees of the cabriole legs are each carved with a lion's mask gripping a ring. Some

Left, Fig. 174: A knee and part of the frieze of the card table in Plate 29.

Below, Fig. 175: Mahogany armchair, the knees carved with satyrs' masks and the arms terminating in eagles' heads. Circa 1745. (Christie's.)

tables of this type were lined on the inside of the top with needlework or fabric, others, like the present example, were polished bare wood and if used for card-playing were doubtless covered with a cloth. Sometimes the polished variety are described as 'tea tables', but there can be no proof of their original purpose and it is probable that they had numerous daily uses.

In chair-making, just as walnut proved to be an enormous advance on oak, so did the introduction of mahogany result in the

Below, *Fig. 176: Walnut chair of similar design to the mahogany armchair in Fig. 175, the knees in the present instance carved with acanthus leaves. Circa 1745. (Parke-Bernet Galleries, Inc.)*

production of chairs of hitherto unattainable grace and durability. The specimen in Fig. 175 shows the intricacy of design that could be realised, with the minimum of wood giving a lightness of appearance allied with strength. A versatile timber, it could be relied upon for ample supplies of consistently good quality. After an unusually hard winter in 1709 European walnut became 'scarce and as a substitute a different variety was brought from North America. It could not compete with mahogany, but even after this had come into general use not every maker deserted walnut. Figs. 176 and 177 show what a really competent craftsman could achieve.

Importation of mahogany was encouraged by the Government allowing it into the country free of duty for a period of 21 years from 1722. Although supplies sent from elsewhere were liable for payment it was dodged:

> The 11th Geo I, cap. 7. imposed a duty of £8 a ton on mahogany of foreign growth imported into Britain; this duty is entirely evaded; for it is brought free into Jamaica, and goes from thence to Britain as Jamaica wood; where, if it sold even at the lowest price, it clears to the shipper nearly the same as the Jamaica cutters.[1]

CABINETS made at the time, *circa* 1735, did not always exploit the versatility of mahogany, and many of them followed the architectural forms introduced by William Kent. The design for a medal cabinet in Fig. 178, was the work of Thomas Langley, brother of the architect Batty Langley, and

[1] *Anonymous*, The History of Jamaica, *3 vols., 1774, quoted by R. W. Symonds, Furniture-making . . ., 1955, page 118.*

a publisher of furniture designs sometimes copied from foreign books which he had the effrontery to claim as his own. The cabinet incorporates many features seen in actual pieces of the period, and the example in Fig. 179 has a comparable simplicity and severity of outline. The gilt applied carving gives it an unusual elegance for its type, and the veneering is also out of the ordinary. Shaped panels of mahogany are bordered by olive-wood which is intersected at intervals by small triangular sections of box; the latter are seen clearly in the photograph on the right-hand side of the door.

The bureau-cabinet illustrated in Fig. 181 is of a more conventional variety, and of later date than the preceding example. It shares with it a serpentine outline of the mouldings on the door, which is a feature found on a number of pieces of furniture attributed to Giles Grendey, of Clerkenwell (see page 188 and Plate 17). It cannot be assumed, however, that the presence of such mouldings, or of a distinctively carved apron like that on a labelled two-stage cupboard,[1] were exclusive to this maker. As in other instances, only the presence of a label or the survival of the original invoice is indisputable evidence.

---

[1] *Heal, op. cit., plates 22–28.*

Below, *Fig. 177: Pair of walnut chairs carved with leaves and scrolls and with hairy claw-and-ball feet. Circa 1750. (Parke-Bernet Galleries, Inc.)*

Plate CLIV.

Medal Cafe

T. Langley Invent & Sculp. 1739.

The balanced proportions of Thomas Langley's 'Medal Case' (Fig. 178) are also seen in the pedestal writing table in Fig. 180. While admiration of a style is a matter of personal taste, the high standard of execution of this piece cannot be denied. The projecting members on the angles, with their sharply cut leaves above rows of discs or 'money', are matched in quality by the leaves, rosettes and other gilt metal mounts.

A number of tables of the same type are in existence, the best-known of them being the one designed, probably by William Kent, for the Earl of Burlington and now at Chatsworth. It has gilt figures of owls at the angles; figures selected because of their

connexion with Athena, Goddess of Learning, and therefore most appropriate for library furniture.

Almost as celebrated is another octagonal pedestal table, also of parcel-gilt mahogany, now in the collection of Her Majesty the Queen, having been acquired in the 1930's by Her Late Majesty Queen Mary.[1] It was originally made for Sir Thomas Robinson, of Rokeby Hall, Yorkshire, and was accompanied by a pair of matching marble-topped three-drawer chests. Their designer is not recorded, but Sir Thomas was an amateur architect, a friend of Lord Burlington and of Kent, and he was responsible for the plan of Rokeby. In view of this, it is not improbable that he may have designed the furniture himself. Regrettably, although he mentioned in a letter written to his father-in-law in 1731 that 'There is now nothing wanting to our reception [at Rokeby], but to put up the furniture which is ready there for that end', he gave no other details.

It was Robinson, incidentally, who wrote of Kent and his extravagant methods and noted that the latter

> often gave his orders when he was full of Claret, and as he did not perhaps see the works for several months after, he had indeed a pretty concise, tho' arbitrary manner to set all right, for he would order without consulting his employers three or four hundred pounds worth of work to be directly pulled down, and then correct the plan to what it ought to have been at first.

The Rokeby table and chests and others comparable with them in appearance and quality have been attributed to the hand of William Vile, who worked for George III and Queen Charlotte. His authorship remains unproved and there is no certainty that they were made by one man or came from a number of different sources, but each is unquestionably the work of a master of his craft.

While carving was usually the favoured decorative medium, a small number of

Right, Fig. 182: Mahogany cabinet inlaid with engraved brass and mounted in gilt metal, the upper drawer pulling forward on corner supports to reveal a writing surface. Attributed to John Channon (see Plate 30). Circa 1745; width 111·7cm. (H. Blairman and Sons.)

makers employed brass inlay. The style was of foreign inspiration, and the name of a German cabinet-maker, Abraham Röntgen, has been linked with its introduction into England. He is known to have been in London between about 1731 and 1738, when he worked for a craftsman named Gern, probably one of his fellow-countrymen, with premises in Clerkenwell. To Röntgen are attributed some pieces of furniture inlaid with brass lines and small shaped engraved plaques of the same metal as well as of mother-of-pearl and ivory. He joined the Moravian sect, was shipwrecked while on his way as a missionary to Carolina and returned to settle at Neuweid, near Cologne. There, his son, David, made fine quality furniture of which a proportion embodies ingenious mechanical features, and although he is not known to have visited the country he described himself as '*Englischer Kabinettmacher*'.

Recent years have seen the emergence of a group of brass-inlaid, gilt-metal-mounted pieces which have a distinction of their own, and would seem to have emanated from a single workshop. The technique of inlaying with metal was developed and popularised in France by the eminent maker André-Charles Boulle, and continued to be employed there by his followers for long after his death in 1732. The dozen or so English works under discussion show, however, unmistakable signs of German inspiration in both their general appearance and their ornamentation.

---

[1] *This table, the foregoing and others are illustrated in* The Dictionary of English Furniture, *revised edition, 1954, vol. III, plate IX and figs. 12, 13, 17 and 21 on pages 245–7.*

The mirror-doored cabinet in Plate 30 has been described as 'one of the most sumptuous surviving pieces of English furniture.'[1] Its delicate brass inlay is decorated with engraving, the metal mounts on the knees and elsewhere are finely designed and finished, and the mahogany from which it is made was most carefully selected for its marking. An unusual feature is that the hinge-plates of the two doors are engraved, each of them with a ram suspended by a belt from entwined snakes and with most of the small remaining space filled with formal leaves. The plates are seen only when the doors are fully opened, and the significance of their ornament has been the subject of speculation.

Further research into the group of furniture led to their comparison with a pair of large bookcases at Powderham Castle, Devonshire. They are made of rosewood inlaid with engraved brass, and 'would not look out of place in an early 18th Century South German Baroque interior'. Stylistic links between the bookcases and the other pieces are clearly present, while of paramount importance is the fact that in the centre of the door frame of each bookcase is a small brass plaque engraved: 'J. Channon Fecit 1740'.

John Channon, it has been discovered,[2] was born in 1711 and baptised at St. Sidwell's Church, Exeter, a half-dozen or so miles from Powderham. At the age of fifteen he was apprenticed to Otho Channon, an Exeter chair-maker who is presumed to have been his elder brother. While the latter remained in his native city, John went to London, where in 1737 he became the occupant of a house in the cabinet-making centre, St. Martin's Lane. His premises, on which he continued paying rates until 1783, were situated in the part of the street known as 'The Pavement', which ran down the west side from about Newport Street to St. Peter's Court. The houses there were set back from the road with a broad walk

Right, *Plate 30: Brass-inlaid mahogany cabinet on stand, attributed to John Channon (1711-?1783) of St. Martin's Lane, London. Circa 1735; width 132.7 cm. (Victoria and Albert Museum.)* **Page 240,** *Fig. 183; Walnut table on cabriole supports with pad feet, the top inlaid in brass with a shaped border line centred on a rosette. Circa 1725; width 91.4 cm. (John Keil, Ltd.)*

before them, hence the name of that section of the Lane.

It is known that Channon's house became No. 109 when street-numbering took place in the 1760's, but the name by which it was known before that event is undiscovered. It may well have been 'At the sign of the Golden Fleece', which would account for the engraving on the hinge plates of the cabinet. That one of the houses, of which there were thirty-eight on the Pavement, bore the name is proved by an advertisement printed in the *London Daily Advertiser* of 16th June 1747, and concluding with the words:

> Enquire at the said house, or at the Golden Fleece on the Pavement of St. Martin's Lane, near Charing Cross.

Whether this was Channon's address or no more than a coincidence has not, as yet, been determined.

It has been suggested that Abraham Röntgen may have collaborated with Channon in making some or all of these pieces of furniture.[3] He was certainly in England at about the right time and practised brass-inlaying, but like many other propositions this one must hopefully await confirmation.

---

[1] *John Hayward, 'English Brass Inlaid Furniture',* in Victoria & Albert Museum Bulletin, *Vol. I, No. 1, January 1965.*

[2] *John Hayward, 'The Channon Family of Exeter and London, Chair and Cabinet Makers',* in Victoria & Albert Museum Bulletin, *Vol. II, No. 2, April 1966.*

[3] *Peter Thornton and Desmond Fitz-Gerald, 'Abraham Rontgen, Englische Kabinettmacher . . .',* in Victoria & Albert Museum Bulletin, *Vol. II, No. 4, October 1966.*

16: The Emergence of the Rococo

Fʀᴏᴍ about the year 1740 there were signs of a change in the shape and decoration of furniture. The simple outlines and limited decorative motifs, all carefully balanced, associated with William Kent and his followers, lost favour. The new fashion was for what was later called the Rococo, which had been introduced earlier in France and was based in part on the forms of rockwork: *rocaille*. An anglicization of the word duly resulted in the term used to designate the style: a style of which the salient features are a deliberate asymmetry and an overall air of fantasy.

Kent employed a limited number of classical motifs arranged formally, whereas there now appeared a wide range of subjects taken from Nature and distributed in a haphazard way. These were unified by a series of curves, most of which were given curled ends so that they resembled a letter 'C'. The ponderous appearance typical of much of the furniture of the decade 1730–40 was succeeded by the complete opposite: a lightness and grace that aimed at movement. The latter was achieved by combining sinuosities of outline and ornament, to which were added not the dead-pan carved masks of the Palladians, but whole-length human figures, animals, and male and female faces wearing animated expressions.

Among the very earliest English representations of Rococo forms were some small books of engraved patterns executed by Matthias Lock and Henry Copland. Although both men were accomplished artists in their own spheres, very little indeed is yet known about their lives. Lock, it is conjectured, was probably the man referred to in an entry in the Apprentice Records of 1724:

> Math [son of] Math [of] St. Paul's Shadwell join[er] to Ric[hard] Goldsaddle of St. Mart/Fields carv[er].

As the majority of boys were then apprenticed at the age of fourteen, it may be inferred that 'Math' Lock was born in or about 1710, and would have served his normal term and been free to set up on his own or seek employment seven years after 1724. Of Richard Goldsaddle no other mention has come to light.

Another contemporaneous mention of the name, not an uncommon one, may also refer to the man in question. In the columns of the *Gentleman's Magazine*, under the heading 'A List of Promotions for Jan. 1737',

discreetly inserted amid a variety of appointments ranging from that of the Duke of Devonshire as Lord-Lieutenant of Ireland to that of Dudley Rider as Attorney-General (see page 165), occurs the entry:

> Mr Lock, —Carpenter to the *Treasury*, in the room of Mr *Willis*, decd.[1]

Proof that the above-quoted records refer to the man under discussion may be forthcoming in due course. Admitting that he served his apprenticeship under Richard Goldsaddle, Matthias Lock would have been aged about thirty when he published in 1740 a set of engravings of which the title-page reads:

> A New Drawing Book of Ornaments, Shields, Compartments, Masks, &c, drawn and engrav'd by M. Lock. Printed for J. Williams, Library of Arts, 10 Charles Street, Soho Square.

The words 'drawn and engrav'd by M. Lock' are misleading as regards all the six plates which make up the compilation. Of them, two are unsigned, while one is inscribed 'F. Vivares fecit' (Fig. 185), and three

'A. Walker sculp'. Francis Vivares was born in France and came to England in about 1727, where he lived in London and became distinguished as an engraver of landscapes. He was married three times, was the father of no fewer than thirty-one children, and died in 1780. On the other hand, Anthony Walker was a native of the British Isles, born at Thirsk, Yorkshire, in 1726, and studied at the St. Martin's Lane Academy, London, which had been founded by William Hogarth in 1735. The Academy was the training-ground of many of the artists who subsequently became exponents of the Rococo.[2]

In the course of the ensuing dozen years Matthias Lock issued several more sets of designs, including *Six Sconces* (mirrors) and *Six Tables* (Fig. 186), in 1744 and 1746

---

[1] *Vol. VII, page 61.*

[2] *See Desmond Fitz-Gerald, 'Chippendale's Place in the English Rococo' in* Furniture History, *IV, 1968, page 1.*

respectively. Both showed actual pieces of furniture, whereas the earlier work had been devoted to a series of sketches in the Rococo manner and their adaptation to practical purposes was left to the craftsman.

Of Henry Copland's career even less is recorded than of Lock's. In 1746 he pub-lished a small volume, little more than a booklet, of which the title-page of one version reads:

A New Book of Ornaments by H. Copland. Price 3s. 6d. Publish'd according to Act of Parliam[t] by Copland in Gutter Lane Cheapside, London.

Other copies state that they were published by 'Copland and Bucksher', while in some all the plates are signed and dated 16 April 1746 and in others this information is absent.

The same title was re-used in 1752, but in place of a series of Rococo fragments and cartouches they were now shown applied to actual pieces of furniture. In addition to announcing this, the title-page stated that the plates were the result of a collaboration. It ran:

> A New Book of Ornaments, with twelve leaves, consisting of chimneys, sconces, tables, spandle pannels,[1] spring clock cases, & stands, a chande-

lier & gerandole &c. By M. Lock and H. Copland. . . .

Another work similarly titled, issued in 1768, bore the imprint of the well-known print-seller of the day, Robert Sayer, while that of 1752 was published by the two authors: Lock 'near yᵉ Swan Tottenham Court Road' and Copland, as before, at Gutter Lane, Cheapside.

The 1768 *New Book of Ornaments* gave the names of the men as 'Matt. Lock and H. Copeland'. In view of this, it may be thought the latter was perhaps the same

---

[1] *Spandrel panels: triangular spaces like those seen at the corners of clock faces.*

Right, *Fig. 188: The title-page from Henry Copland's* A New Book of Ornaments, *1746.*

Below, *Fig. 187: Carved, gilded and painted side table, designed and carved by Matthias Lock for Hinton House, Hinton St. George, Somerset.* Circa 1745; width 152·4 cm. *(Sotheby's.)*

person who appeared in a book-list issued by J. Millan, whose premises were 'opposite the Admiralty'. In the 1761 edition of *Millan's Universal Register* the index was followed by a leaf of 'Books printed for J. Millan', of which item 23 reads:

Millan's Peerage of England, Scotland and Ireland, and Baronets, finely engraved by Mr. Copeland. 15s.

Equally, Copland may have been the subject of a tantalizingly brief obituary notice in the *London Magazine* in 1761 (Vol. XXX, page 332): 'June 5 Mr. Copeland, an eminent engraver.'

Copland also engraved a design for a chair in a volume published in 1766,[1] but this could have been executed earlier and put aside until a convenient occasion arose for its use. The engraving bears only his signature and the absence of a date means that this could have taken place, so it does not invalidate the possibility that he died in 1761.

WHILE Henry Copland is known only as a designer and engraver, Matthias Lock was both a designer and an accomplished wood-carver. In the International

---

[1] The Chair-Maker's Guide, *by Robert Manwaring. See P. Ward-Jackson, op. cit., page 53 and plates 181–183.*

New Book of
Ornaments
BY
H. Copland
Price 5ˢ 6ᵈ

Publish'd according to Act of Parliam't by Copland

in Gutter Lane Cheapside London.

Exhibition held in London in 1862, one of the items displayed was a collection of Lock's drawings which was shown by his grandson, George Lock, of Edinburgh. They, and others, were purchased by the Museum of Ornamental Art, now the Victoria and Albert Museum, and among them are some rough sketches and memoranda relating to work he had carried out. One of them, illustrated in Fig. 184, shows a carved console table. It is headed *A Table in ye Tapestry Roome*, and lists the names of those who worked on the piece, the length of time each expended on it, and details of the cost:

Days.		£	s	d
89 in all	Joyner	1	5	0
Lock 15	Carving 21 :	0 .	0	
Loman 20 [?Lomax]				
Hill 10				
Wood [?] 15 the others				
time &c				

The final words, 'the others time &c' presumably refers to the difference between the total of 89 days and the 60 days allocated to the four named craftsmen. For the matching candle-stands (Fig. 189) there is a similar gap of 52 days.

Two other sketches of the same type refer also to the Tapestry Room: one *A Large Sconce* and the other *Two Stands*. The location of all these pieces was discovered in 1960, and revealed as being Hinton House, Hinton St. George, Somerset, seat of the Earls Poulett.[1] Since that date, the furniture has been dispersed, but the table and 'sconce' are now in the Victoria and Albert Museum (Plate 31). The suite was probably made for the second earl shortly after he succeeded to the title in 1743.

Lock's notes make no mention of gilding, which may have been carried out by a specialist and have been the subject of a separate transaction, or was not added at the time. The gilding seen on the pieces today was done in the 19th Century at the same time as they were parcel-bronzed, and

Á. Copland. Fecit et dp. 1746

Left, *Fig. 189: Detail of one of a pair of candle-stands, gilded and partly bronzed, designed and carved by Matthias Lock. Circa 1745. (Sotheby's.)*

Above, *Fig. 190: Rococo design, from Copland's* New Book of Ornaments.

it is uncertain whether the work was a restoration or entirely new.

It may be added that the 'Large Sconce' occupied Lock alone twenty days and his three assistants considerably more, and the cost totalled £36. 5s. Of this sum, the carving accounted for £34. 10s. The stands were the most expensive of all at £50 the pair, and their making occupied no less than 188 days. In this instance the carving of each of them cost £23. 10s., the joiner's work £1, and that of the turner 10s.

[1] J. F. Hayward, *'Furniture designed and carved by Matthias Lock for Hinton House, Somerset'*, in The Connoisseur, *December 1960, p. 284.*

A further reference to Matthias Lock came to light in 1964 with the finding of a scrap of paper among some documents at Hopetoun House, West Lothian, seat of the Marquess of Linlithgow. Undated, and no longer with the sketches originally accompanying it, which must have been returned for the use of the carver, it reads:

> The enclosed drawings are valuable being designed and drawn by the famous Mr Matt Lock recently deceased who was reputed the best Draftsman in that way that had ever been in England.

The note has been identified as probably referring to a set of four pier-glasses which are still at Hopetoun House.[1] They were, it has been suggested, provided 'in 1766' by the London cabinet-maker James Cullen,

'after being designed by Matthias Lock and carved and gilded by Samuel Norman'. The date is apparently based on a letter of 22 May 1766 written by Cullen, in which he estimates the cost of supplying both glass and frames, but there is no evidence of when the articles were actually delivered.

The oval-shaped frames are in the newly-introduced neo-classic style, as are the designs in Lock's pattern-book of 1769. This was:

A New Book of Pier-Frame's, Oval's, Gerandole's, Tables, &c.

If the glasses at Hopetoun House were

---

[1] *A Coleridge,* Chippendale Furniture, *1968, pages 164–5 and plate 411.*

delivered in 1766 and the note refers to them, then this was a posthumous publication.

In 1955 it was stated that 'the liveliness and technical skill of Lock have not been sufficiently appreciated: he is one of the best draughtsmen of the designers whose drawings survive from the middle of the century.'[1] Since then, more study has been devoted to him, and the appearance of some of his documented work at auction in London has confirmed public appreciation of his merit. Sotheby's sold the pair of candle-stands from Hinton House (Fig. 189) on 1st November 1968 for no less than £23,000. This was certainly an exceptional price, but with few other pieces of furniture is it possible to trace so many details of their making or know that they had been in the house for which they were made for an unbroken period of about 225 years.

The design of the Hinton suite shows a bold use of masks and leaves, and although they are arranged in the formal fashion of 1730–40 Lock's skill has given them a liveliness absent from the work of his contemporaries. Nonetheless, it will be seen that they exhibit no trace of the Rococo dominant in his *New Drawing Book of Ornaments*, which had been published in 1740 (Fig. 185). His client's taste was for the well-tried, and the Earl, who was about thirty-five years of age in 1743 when he probably furnished his Tapestry Room, apparently did not wish to be a pioneer in the matter of

---

[1] *R. Edwards and M. Jourdain, op. cit., page 60.*

taste. This might have been acceptable in the case of a London house, but was perhaps misplaced in the heart of Somerset as the background for a bachelor who served as Lord-Lieutenant of the county for twenty years.

Matthias Lock's set of engraved plates, *Six Tables*, was issued on 10 April 1746, precisely six days before Copland's *Ornaments* (Figs. 188 and 190). One of the tables is shown in Fig. 186, and is accompanied by

a variety of alternative details. All of them show the Rococo at its most asymmetrical, and include such elements as 'icicles' or 'dripping water', shells, 'tongues of flame', dragons, dolphins and masks, and the inevitable 'C'-scrolls and flowers. The table which is of the console type for affixing to a wall, is very close in pattern to French examples of the time. It may be noticed that each of the legs differs from the other, so that a buyer or maker could select from

Left, *Fig. 193: Reading chair on which the user sits astride and faces the back, sometimes known as a 'cock-fighting' chair. Circa 1740. (Sotheby's.)*

Below, *Fig. 194: Carved mahogany settee, the back and seat covered in gros- and petit-point needlework. Circa 1740; width 160 cm. (Christie's.)*

them which he preferred. The knees might be ornamented either with dragons or with bearded masks, the latter bearing a distinct resemblance to the young George Bernard Shaw!

Lock and Copland's 1752 *New Book of Ornaments* shows the two men making full use of a complete understanding of the Rococo. The designs in Fig. 191 are for an overmantel glass and one to hang on a wall, both of them basically formed of 'C'-scrolls which are almost overwhelmed by a profusion of floral sprigs and garlands, and pierced curling 'flames'. In addition, there is a Chinese musician as well as the head of a person (European, Chinese?) wearing a pagoda-shaped hat, and an exotic bird; all of which were to be seen with increasing frequency during the coming years.

A charge levelled sometimes at the work of many of the Rococo designers is that their drawings or engraved work would seem to be impossibly difficult to translate into fact. There are, however, many examples of this having been achieved with success; in some instances closely following the original and in others with modifications to suit the taste and ability of the maker. The oval looking-glass in Fig. 192 has been adapted from the right-hand example in the Lock and Copland engraving in Fig. 191. The result may be adjudged heavier in appearance than the latter, but allowance must be made for the ease with which the engraver's needle runs over copper; the technique of using a chisel on wood is very different. The variations between the published pattern and this specimen of the finished article may indicate that the frame is the work of someone other than Lock, who might have been expected to follow his own (or rather, his and Copland's) design closely. As regards the latter's share, he would have confined his attention to drawing and engraving, for there is no evidence whatsoever that he worked with wood either as a joiner or a carver.

The period 1740–50 was one in which the

craft of the carver came to the fore. His skill was encouraged by the virtues of mahogany, which almost completely displaced walnut for the making of all types of articles. The settee in Fig. 194 is typical of many of the formal pieces of the time, with its upright back and deep seat promising little in the way of satisfying comfort. On the other hand, it is highly decorative in appearance and a minor triumph on the parts of joiner, carver and embroiderer, while it will be noticed that it shows no trace of Rococo. The arms terminate in open-mouthed lions' heads, the shallow apron is decorated with Vitruvian scrolls which meet in the centre, while the cabriole legs bear a pattern of vine leaves and curled foliage on the knees and terminate in lions' paw feet grasping balls. The seat and back are covered in gros- and petit-point needlework, the back having a central panel showing a procession of Oriental figures.

Unorthodox in looks, but again showing an unawareness of Rococo, and certainly for informal use is the chair in Fig. 193. It is of a type on which the user sits astride facing the back and was once, and often still is, termed a 'cock-fighting' chair. The back has an adjustable book-rest, there are pen compartments in the curved arms, and in the apron is a cupboard reached by a pair of doors. The four cabriole legs are quite plain with pad feet, and there are stretchers linking them to the pair of turned back legs

which prevent the chair toppling over when in use. It is covered in red leather held in place and trimmed with round-headed brass nails, which were frequently used for the purpose at that date.

The armchair in Fig. 195 is of conventional type, but has some less usual features. In the majority of instances the arm-supports sweep forward as in Plate 32, but here they curve back from the curled ends and are carved with acanthus leaves. The cabriole legs are similarly ornamented and terminate in rounded feet somewhat resembling horses' hooves.

Below, *Fig. 195: Carved walnut armchair with rounded 'pad' feet. Circa 1740. (John Keil, Ltd.)*

INDEX

All references are to page numbers, those to the text in roman type and to the illustrations in *italic*.